PRAISE FOR *ACCELERATED DIGITAL TRANSFORMATION*

T0293714

"Chopra's new book helps you reduce bad friction into a manageable hexagon comb while introducing good friction to sweeten the honey from digital transformation."
Soon Yu, Author, Friction: *Adding Value by Making People Work For It*

"We live in a time where the fog of technology is often overwhelming, difficult to dissect and changing so rapidly it becomes difficult to have confidence in our decision making. Neetan Chopra takes the mystery out of creating successful digital transformations for companies and their clients in a way that brings light and clarity to an otherwise challenging process. The insights he has gathered through his years of technology experience provide the keys for those who are looking to unlock value during these extraordinary times."
Tim Kobe, Founder and CEO, Eight Inc.

"Every enterprise must succeed on a digital journey to remain relevant, serve customers and add value. *Accelerated Digital Transformation* provides you with a pragmatic guide and framework to achieve progress and success. I appreciate Neetan Chopra's storytelling approach and many lessons of everyday role models delivering extraordinary customer service. These stories demonstrate the Uplifting Service ethos that earns customer praise and social media attention."
Ron Kaufman, New York Times Bestselling Author, *Uplifting Service: The Proven Path to Delighting Your Customers, Colleagues, and Everyone Else You Meet*

"Only if one has lived through or, even better, driven digital transformation of a major company, can one seriously understand what it means to write a book about it that is worth reading. Neetan Chopra is exactly one of these few leaders who has lived through such digital transformations and knows exactly what it means, what works and what doesn't. Chopra's book is probably one of the very few books about digital transformation really worth reading, as it is not yet another consultant textbook, far remote from reality, but written by true experience and painful learnings."
Patrick Naef, Managing Partner, Boyden

"*Accelerated Digital Transformation* deftly fuses practical examples and actionable insights from Neetan Chopra's vast digital experience, with deep foundational learning, borne out of his global academic pursuits. Chopra's storytelling approach, coupled with innovative interventions, such as co-authoring a chapter with an

AI-bot, make the book both engaging and first-of-a-kind read. We highly recommend this book, for anyone looking to navigate the ever-evolving digital landscape and staying ahead of the game in the digital era."

Prof Dr Reinhard Jung, Dean, School of Management, University of St Gallen

Prof Dr Ulrike Baumöl, Executive Director, Executive MBA HSG in Business Engineering, University of St Gallen

"Having seen first-hand how Neetan Chopra executes successful digital transformation where others have struggled, I am grateful he has taken the time to write down his framework. His deliberate 'cell-by-cell' strategy is what it takes to assess, learn and succeed in this complicated mix of technical, business and cultural transformation. And a bonus, he demonstrates learning with this framework by co-authoring one chapter with an AI bot... brilliant!"

Jana Eggers, CEO, Nara Logics

"All transformations, digital or otherwise, are in essence a human journey of change. I like Chopra's storytelling, a colloquial approach to the intimidating topic of digital transformation for business leaders. This will connect with people across all walks of life, demystifying what it takes to thrive in the digital era and create exponential outcomes. The six global experts, the honeycomb archetypes, provide an additional human touch, sharing their experiences and wisdom, using Chopra's *Accelerated Digital Transformation* as a platform. A must read."

Raj Jain, Former CEO, Bennett Coleman & Co Limited (Times Group)

"Organizations need simple frameworks by which they can plan their digital transitions. Neetan Chopra's efforts on achieving this through a well thought out 'Honeycomb Framework' is commendable. His building blocks of digital transformation provide a succinct and clear framework through which readers can apply these in the context of their organizations. The future is about organizations which will survive and thrive in a digitally driven business ecosystem. Chopra's book will help organizations survive and thrive in a VUCA world.'

Krishnakumar Natarajan, Co-founder & Former Executive Chairperson, LTIMindtree

"An insightful, practitioners' guide full of pragmatic ideas and valuable learnings from decades of experience. A must-read for executives vying for industry leadership in digital."

Joydeep Sengupta, Senior Partner, McKinsey & Company

"More than 80% of digital transformation projects fail inside large organizations, not through lack of trying. Every organization looking to crack the code for success should read Neetan Chopra's book. By taking a practitioner's point of view, he draws from three decades of experience to provide a proven methodology known as the Honeycomb Framework. *Accelerated Digital Transformation* is a must-read book for digital leaders."

R 'Ray' Wang, Founder and Chairman, Constellation Research

Accelerated Digital Transformation

*How established organizations can gain
competitive advantage in the digital age*

Neetan Chopra

KoganPage

Publisher's note

Every possible effort has been made to ensure that the information contained in this book is accurate at the time of going to press, and the publishers and authors cannot accept responsibility for any errors or omissions, however caused. No responsibility for loss or damage occasioned to any person acting, or refraining from action, as a result of the material in this publication can be accepted by the editor, the publisher or the author.

First published in Great Britain and the United States in 2023 by Kogan Page Limited

Apart from any fair dealing for the purposes of research or private study, or criticism or review, as permitted under the Copyright, Designs and Patents Act 1988, this publication may only be reproduced, stored or transmitted, in any form or by any means, with the prior permission in writing of the publishers, or in the case of reprographic reproduction in accordance with the terms and licences issued by the CLA. Enquiries concerning reproduction outside these terms should be sent to the publishers at the undermentioned addresses:

2nd Floor, 45 Gee Street
London
EC1V 3RS
United Kingdom

8 W 38th Street, Suite 902
New York, NY 10018
USA

4737/23 Ansari Road
Daryaganj
New Delhi 110002
India

www.koganpage.com

Kogan Page books are printed on paper from sustainable forests.

© Neetan Chopra, 2022

The right of Neetan Chopra to be identified as the author of this work has been asserted by him in accordance with the Copyright, Designs and Patents Act 1988.

ISBNs

Hardback   978 1 3986 0894 8
Paperback   978 1 3986 0892 4
Ebook   978 1 3986 0893 1

British Library Cataloguing-in-Publication Data

A CIP record for this book is available from the British Library.

Library of Congress Control Number

2023000253

Typeset by Integra Software Services, Pondicherry
Print production managed by Jellyfish
Printed and bound by CPI Group (UK) Ltd, Croydon CR0 4YY

CONTENTS

LIST OF FIGURES

PREFACE

The enterprise world is in turmoil.

The digital era hit this world hard and fast. Just yesterday, the legacy incumbents were in positions of complete dominance. And then, in the blink of an eye, threatened, vulnerable, perplexed. For long durations of the industrial era, they basked at the top of market cap charts. The stock market's top echelons are now totally dominated by digital natives. (Today, 8 out of the top 10 companies by market cap are digital companies.[1]) Once a magnet for top talent and lifetime commitment, now they are bystanders to an explosion of entrepreneurial and digital career options.

Grand View Research estimates the global digital transformation market size to be between $350 and $450 billion and growing at a rapid clip of CAGR 22.5 per cent from 2020 to 2027.[2] Digital transformation, with its nearly half-a-trillion-dollar market size, is not a fad.[3] It is real, it is here to stay, and it profoundly impacts individuals, enterprises and societies. Catch up with any CEO of any business, in any industry, any geography, and digital will appear in their top three strategic priorities.

For large legacy enterprises, digital disruption posed an existential challenge even pre-pandemic, but the threat was more in the medium-to-long term. In the wake of Covid, there has been a quantum time collapse. Digital became urgent to survival as lockdowns kicked revenues into a steep abyss. Doing digital helped companies stay afloat. However, to thrive in the digital era, enterprises need to *be* digital instead of just *do* digital. Being digital is inherent to digital natives, yet so far and alien to the enterprise world!

A case in point is the retail industry. What's common to Sears, JCPenney, Barneys, Toys R Us, Brooks Brothers, GNC? They were all household names, loved by consumers globally. And now they are all gone. Kaput! Bankrupt! The year 2020 was a record one for retail store closures in the US. An unprecedented 12,200 stores, big and small, closed shop in 2020 after 10,000 had done so in 2019.[4] The retail world is going through a digital apocalypse. I am sure the CEOs of these premier brands realized the existential crises they faced from Amazon or numerous other nimble online retailers. These leaders would have loved to find some of that Amazon.com DNA, including its deeply embedded passion for customers. However, as this apocalypse amply demonstrates, disruption from within does not come easy.

So much has changed in such a short time for these humble incumbents. Most CEOs fully realize the existential crises they face. They desire so genuinely to disrupt before being disrupted; to get ahead of the curve; to digitally disrupt; to save these corporate legends, the who's who of yesteryears, now slowly bound toward the graveyard of legacy. However, there are not many examples of incumbent enterprises achieving digital disruption or even getting close, despite this authentic desire.

You may ask, what is the reason? Why aren't the incumbents achieving exponential results? Despite their deep pockets, why are they unable to shift the needle? Why is it that most progress is most visible only in the olive branches of corporate annual reports? Why do significant big-bang transformation initiatives not see the light at the end of a very long tunnel? Why are CEOs and their CDOs struggling to make meaningful, sustainable transformation of their enterprises? This predominantly relates to the *how* of transformation.

This book is an insider's guide to transformation from within. It is about the *how* of authentic digital transformation. This book is not about the how for the Ubers, the Airbnbs, or the numerous other slick digital start-ups. The Honeycomb approach is about the how for our legacy incumbents, the industrial era enterprise, the asset-heavy operating model, the linear business models, the legacy yet aspirant mindset, the humble incumbents of the industrial era.

This book is about helping the enterprise world unlock the potential for success in the digital era. I do not aspire to provide a panacea, as there is none. Each journey of transformation is different. However, from my experience of engaging deeply with this topic within large enterprises, I aspire to provide a better guide for disruption than the random executive tourism to HQs of digital natives – a better toolset than those garnered from isolated digital transformation conferences. I have consolidated my experience and the learning from a vast global network into a unique framework, an assistant, a coach and a guide to help executives meaningfully transform their enterprises for success in the digital era. I call this framework the Honeycomb.

FIGURE 0.1 Honeycomb in a box

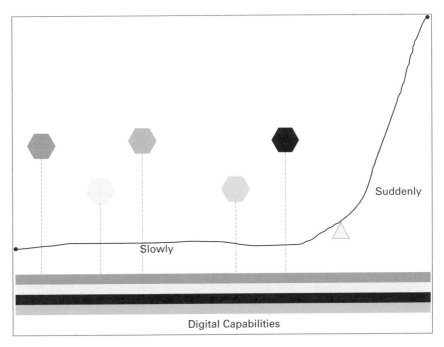

The hypothesis underpinning the Honeycomb is simple. How does one transform a large, incumbent enterprise? You do it by following the exponential curve. The change happens slowly at first, and then, suddenly (see Figure 0.1). You do it by taking one carefully chosen organizational cell (any division of an enterprise, such as marketing or IT) at a time and re-imagining it. You do it by connecting each re-imagined initiative to a foundational set of core digital capabilities. You do that with pace as your best friend in this journey.

The digital transformation will reach a tipping point when the system of re-imagined organizational cells connect in harmony. The organization will organically, and so suddenly, move up the exponential curve of performance. A complete disruption. A complete transformation – like that of a caterpillar into a butterfly – into a new world of sustainable exponential outcomes and performance.

I invite you to this journey through the Honeycomb.

Writing a book on disruption should also disrupt the writing of the book! Hence the book is organized into two main parts. In the first part, I share my experience of leading large-scale digital transformations, encapsulated into the Honeycomb framework. This is the standard 'Honeycomb as an author' paradigm. Throughout the book, I have peppered the explanation of the framework with personal stories from my experience of leading such transformation initiatives within large enterprises.

How this book is structured

In Chapter 1, *Legacy enterprises equal inertia*, And these companies and their leaders have proper reasons for this inertia. First, the enterprise has an existing revenue stream, which contributes good EBITDA (earnings before interest, taxes, depreciation, and amortization) This needs to be protected. A large customer base expects and pays for existing products, services and experiences.

Corporate governance, audit and compliance, regulatory pressures, media, analysts, activists – the repertoire of barriers that cement the inertia are deep and wide. So, executives suck it in and carry on with their good lives using time-tested clichés such as 'why fix what ain't broken?'. Before you can disrupt, you need to jolt the enterprise out of its comfort zone. In Chapter 1, *Breaking organizational inertia*, I describe my personal story of doing precisely that and creating the initial momentum for transformation in a large enterprise.

Chapter 2, *Working the Honeycomb – disrupt phase*, and Chapter 3, *Working the Honeycomb – digital capabilities*, detail the two vectors of the Honeycomb framework. The disrupt phase is 'what you do' to the six nodes of every organization cell, one cell at a time. The capabilities phase is 'what you leave behind', for disruption to nurture and grow forever. Get inspired with stories such as that of Chris and the Hatman, which brings to life topics such as customer obsession and how it needs to percolate into the organization's soul instead of just staying perched on top of fancy mission statements. Or the story of Move37 – a divine and inspired move by an AI bot that highlights how a disruptive technology can impact the world. These chapters captures the essence of the Honeycomb framework, including the stories from my experiences in driving digital transformation, which anchor the framework to real-life contexts.

In Chapter 4, *Accelerated possibilities*, I cover four broad areas: business model disruption, antifragile leadership, autonomous ops, and algorithmic marketing and sales. I cover the explosion of business models that have occurred in the digital era. Disney shifted from selling family entertainment to selling experiences. User-generated content disrupted content creation, giving birth to new enterprises such as YouTube and Vimeo. The 'as a service' business model was born, and even products such as razors were converted to 'shave as a service' by digital natives like Dollar Shave Club. I dive into platform business models, which behemoths such as

Amazon and Alibaba have used to gain market dominance. I offer practical insights into how leaders can become antifragile in the wake of immense volatility. I bust common leadership myths around technology. Finally, I show how the Honeycomb framework uncovers the art of the possible for the back-office operations and front-end marketing, sales, and customer engagement functions of a large enterprise.

As I was penning this book, humanity faced one of its biggest challenges ever – the Covid-19 pandemic. Lenin said, 'There are decades when nothing happens, and then there are weeks when decades happen.' This postulation came to life during the pandemic, when digital transformation efforts across industries across the globe were accelerated. Chapter 4, *Accelerated possibilities*, brings out areas and examples of where Covid has significantly accelerated digital disruption. It inks this acceleration to the Honeycomb approach, where appropriate. The chapter also covers how critical aspects of the Honeycomb approach and framework such as invisible ops, customer obsession, radical digitization, AI and data helped companies stay afloat during the pandemic. It brings out how these capabilities were sorely missed by those who still treat digital transformation as a fad.

The Honeycomb approach recommends experimenting with and adopting new digital business models continuously. For example, fitness companies and gyms closed as the pandemic hit, but some fitness studios, such as New York-based Fhitting Room, were able to pivot to digital classes and grow their corporate business through the pandemic.[5]

In the second part of the book, in Chapter 5, *Honeycomb as a platform*, I take inspiration from the predominant business model disrupter of the digital era – platforms. This part is the Honeycomb as a platform paradigm. In this part, the book becomes a platform orchestrator, wherein I have assimilated the experiences and wisdom of six top-notch disrupters from my global network. They represent six different perspectives and archetypes: The Thinker (Michiel),

The Coach (Lee Ann), The Clairvoyant (Paul), The Professor (Dr Stuart), The Realist (Radha) and last, but definitely not the least, The Outlier (Mittu). These are leaders and experts in my network with real-life experience in driving change and transformation.

Professor Stuart is a Distinguished Service Professor at Carnegie Mellon University, Silicon Valley. Stuart's professional career spans across many areas of entrepreneurship, featuring extensive experience within the tech ecosystem of Silicon Valley. He has conducted research for SRI International and Stanford Graduate School of Business, consulted with Bain and Company, worked in investing for Sand Hill Venture Group, and served as executive management for Shugart Corporation, a Xerox subsidiary. Michiel is the Global Chief Technology Officer of Sogeti, based in Amsterdam, and is well known for his research on the impact of technology on society. Michiel has formulated the concept of 'un-organization', which lays down a framework for how incumbent enterprises should respond to the threat from digital natives. Paul had a long stint with the CIA, after which he was an executive educator at Thunderbird School of Global Management (where he is now an Emeritus faculty member). Paul focuses on helping senior executives and their organizations understand how to navigate the challenges and opportunities posed by the powerful mega-trends driving today's fast-moving, highly disruptive, complex and ambiguous global business environment. Lee Ann has coached hundreds of Fortune 1000 leaders from over 50 countries to uncover their unique genius, bridge the divides that hold them back from transformative growth, and accelerate positive impact in their leadership and lives. Radha is presently the Executive Chairperson of a new-age start-up, Flutura Decision Sciences and Analytics, and over the years has worked on strategy, market acceleration, value creation and in navigating the nuances of digital transformation. Mittu is a board-level business and technology leader who has helped define, drive, scale-up and deliver four digital transformation journeys. His last transformation journey was with a scale-up, Careem, which was successfully sold to Uber for $3.1 billion.[6]

The concluding thoughts have been jointly co-authored by me and an AI bot, in Chapter 6, *The Honeycomb hacks*, as a set of hacks. As Michiel, our Thinker archetype shares with us, AI has become a general-purpose technology, with profound impact expected from it in all spheres of life. Hence, I enlisted the help of our AI brethren to help summarize some of the learnings from the Honeycomb journey.

In Chapter 7, *Reflections*, I have shared key aspects, learning and setbacks from my digital career, spanning three decades. I categorize my experience into three distinct phases digital–transactional, digital–strategic and digital–transformation. While the entire Honeycomb approach encapsulates my digital–transformation experience, in this chapter I have shared the relevant learnings from the first two phases leading up to transformation.

The Honeycomb framework

Frameworks are like good red wine. They add zero practical value when ensconced in a cask or bottle. They flourish when you get them out, smell those grapes and taste that pure magic on your expectant palate. As I share below the Honeycomb approach, keep this thought of practical applicability at the fore of your mind. All frameworks are only helpful if the underpinning approach is actually applied to your business and your context.

The Honeycomb approach takes its inspiration from two well-known natural phenomena – the honeycomb and the exponential curve. The honeycomb teaches us to create exponential change one cell at a time. A honeycomb's hexagonal structure has the strength to hold the most amount of material with the least amount of wax.[7] Strength and efficiency are two attributes of this beautiful organic structure, so well-known to bees. They create their honeycomb storage for the honey and home for their young ones, together assembling one cell at a time, and the result is a genuinely transformational structure.

The exponential curve is the inspiration behind my belief that enterprise transformation using the Honeycomb disruption method will happen slowly first and then suddenly. The sudden upsurge in performance will emerge automatically, naturally, organically. A set of digital capabilities will enable this surge – capabilities that need to be incubated and nurtured. While the disruption of each cell is itself significant and worthy of enter-prise-wide celebration, the 'difference that makes the difference' lies in the connectivity of the outcomes of each cell to the under-pinning digital capability fabric of the enterprise. If you do not get that one right, you get isolated improvements. If you get the cell and the underpinning capabilities in accordance, you get a mean-ingful transformation.

Overall, the framework comprises two key phases, happening in parallel.

1 The disrupt phase, wherein we transform the cells of an enterprise's existing operating model one cell at a time.
2 The capability phase, where we link these disrupt initiatives to a set of digital capabilities, creating the nurturing ground for expo-nential performance to emerge.

When applied to the context of an existing business model, this approach results in exponential performance within the enter-prise. When applied to the context of a new market/product/service, it results in the birth of new, digitally native business models.

However, before these two phases can kick into high gear, there is a vital need to break the organizational inertia and create momentum for the transformation within an inertia-loving, large enterprise. This is done in three steps:

- Step one is to apply a force.
- Step two is to develop a disruptive vision.

- Step three is immersion of the upper echelons of the enterprise into that vision.

This is the prelude to the Honeycomb. This is when the enterprise takes the first plunge to leave the shores of its comfort zone and break through the organizational inertia.

Endnotes

1 Largest companies by market cap (2022). https://companiesmarketcap.com/ (archived at https://perma.cc/CD2W-3KZ8)

2 Grand View Research (2022) 'Digital transformation market size, share & trends analysis report by solution (analytics, cloud computing, social media, mobility), by service, by deployment, by enterprise, by end use, by region, and segment forecasts, 2022–2030'. www.grandviewresearch.com/industry-analysis/digital-transformation-market (archived at https://perma.cc/37EE-R887) 2

3 Saldanha, T. (2022) 'Why successful digital transformation is a trillion dollar opportunity?', CEO Insights. www.ceoinsightsindia.com/tech-leader-talks/why-successful-digital-transformation-is-a-trillion-dollar-opportunity-nwid-1355.html (archived at https://perma.cc/WXF6-WZN6)

4 Wahba, P. (2021) 'A record 12,200 U.S. stores closed in 2020 as e-commerce, pandemic changed retail forever', *Fortune*, 7 January. fortune.com/2021/01/07/record-store-closings-bankruptcy-2020/ (archived at https://perma.cc/GB9G-RKVU)

5 Barkho, G. (2021) 'As the pandemic continues, gyms are pivoting to virtual corporate perks', *ModernRetail*, 13 January. www.modernretail.co/retailers/gyms-are-pivoting-to-virtual-corporate-perks/ (archived at https://perma.cc/649U-TTMN)

6 Alrawi, M. (2020) 'Uber completes $3.1 billion deal to buy Dubai's Careem', *The National News*, 5 January. www.thenationalnews.com/business/uber-completes-3-1-billion-deal-to-buy-dubai-s-careem-1.959406#:~:text=Uber%20completed%20the%20%243.1%20billion,subsidiary%20of%20the%20American%20firm (archived at https://perma.cc/5HF6-N4EQ)

7 George, S (2017) 'Why are honeycomb cells hexagonal?', *Science Friday*, 1 September. www.sciencefriday.com/educational-resources/why-do-bees-build-hexagonal-honeycomb-cells/ (archived at https://perma.cc/NY75-Y4GQ)

01

Breaking organizational inertia

Larger enterprises equal inertia. It is not easy to change anything, let alone transform the entire enterprise. Resistance is most ingrained in legacy mindsets. Executives kill ideas before they can take shape because 'they were not invented here'. People are enamoured by credentials as opposed to capabilities and merit. Teams want to do everything themselves as opposed to co-creating with the world. Power in large enterprises comes from hoarding information as opposed to democratizing it. Leaders are perpetually full of themselves as opposed to inspiring others and spreading the surface area of leadership. The list of legacy mindset attributes goes on and on.

And there is a proper reason for this inertia. First, the enterprise has an existing revenue stream that contributes good EBITDA (earnings before interest, taxes, depreciation and amortization). This needs to be protected. The enterprise has a large customer base that expects and pays for existing products, services and experiences. Inertia is further cemented by a number of regulatory, legal, behavioural barriers including corporate governance, audit and compliance, regulatory pressures, media, analysts and activists. So, executives suck it in and carry on with their good lives using time-tested clichés such as 'why fix what ain't broken?'.

Step one – apply a force

To get the enterprise out of this inertia, you need to apply a force in order to build internal momentum within the enterprise. I had the good fortune of leading the transformation journey in a large aviation enterprise. Let me share that story.

It was December in Dubai, and the weather was just perfect. As part of my IT Governance role, the next IT steering board meeting was due just before the year's sunset. The agenda of the board meeting was quite innocuous, and I was feeling alright. Although there is always a butterfly in your stomach when you run such meetings, irrespective of your number of years into doing so. After all, the board comprises the crème da le crème, top brass, of this large, global multi-billion-dollar aviation group. The meeting went well and we were about to announce closure, when one of our presidents suddenly announced that he wanted to table an item which was not on the original agenda! The butterflies, by now in standby mode, suddenly started getting a bit restless.

What transpired was quite inspirational. Our president described in simple business terms the external context of the digital era and asked us to prepare a business strategy and plan to respond to it. It was a simple discourse from a sharp executive who sensed a tectonic change and wanted to be ahead of the curve. The mandate for running this initiative fell in my lap. Serendipity in full action. In this case, the force came from one of the executives sensing the winds of disruption and then commissioning an evaluation and strategy to cope with it. The year was 2013, so there was not much traction within large enterprises on digital transformation and its potential. Hence, it was quite exemplary that the force came internally from the top executive of a successful enterprise.

Several years later, the C-suite of a diversified group of companies in a completely different industry than aviation was well aware of digital transformation and its impact. Hence the force (or burning platform as some like to call it) was created by me.

I built the case for disruption based on (a) threat to existing business models and the (b) exponential opportunity digital represents. In some other cases, the force could be an external event such as a change of CEO, sharp dip in performance of the company or sharp dip in market share to a digital native. What is key here is the force. If it does not exist organically, your job as a disrupter is to create it. The force could be based on threat or opportunity, or both. Once the force slightly shakes up the inertia, the next step is to create a compelling, disruptive vision.

Step two – develop a disruptive vision

Going back to the story, after the board minutes were issued, I started looking at the last item on the document and scratching my head on what to do next. There was no clear playbook on leading digital transformations. I am still not sure there is one. Since invention is born out of necessity, we created our own playbook. The first step was to onboard a co-disrupter into the initiative. I firmly believe in this concept of *co*-founders invented by the start-up world. Two is better than one, and three is a crowd. So, I teamed up with someone in the commercial business unit with deep domain knowledge of the aviation business, but more importantly, an open, curious and passionate mindset to be able to disrupt it. In a transformation journey it is best to follow passion as opposed to just expertise or set norms.

Our first action was to assemble divisional heads from core functions, explain the context to them and ask for their inputs. Next, we organized a nice dinner in a lovely Dubai restaurant. Over good food, we shared the task given to us by the IT steering board. Then, we went around the table to get each leader's perspective and guidance on the next steps. What followed was two hours of chatter. There was strong pushback from some quarters. What exactly are we trying to do here? Our revenue is good; our EBIDTA is tracking well against budgets – what is wrong with our existing business and operating models? Why should we fix what ain't broken? Some others had a level of alignment with the mission to 're-imagine the aviation business from the lens of digital' but had no idea how to go about it. There was a lot of discussion, but not much clarity on what and how at the end of the meeting.

Subsequently, we decided that this was a unique initiative with not much of a heuristic available, and hence we needed to craft a pathway of our own. The roadmap needed to be organic, based on sensing the activities done, evaluating the outcome and crafting the next steps. Not command and control architecture based on past norms, but a sense and respond pathway built on the adaptability principle. We knew that as a next step we needed a captivating vision on which we could anchor our transformation initiative, align key stakeholders, and inspire the vital many in the workforce.

We decided to unleash a firehose of ideas for the core of our business and then craft an exponential vision of the future based on these ideas. I was looking for a deeper re-imagination of the core aspects of the airline business and then crafting the potential future state for each core domain. I wanted to uncover the art of the possible – not just for the edges, but for core domains such as airline pricing, distribution, customer engagement, back office. Once you get to the heart of commercial and operational value chains, you get interest from key stakeholders. It might be negative and cynical interest, but it is interest, nevertheless. In addition, we ensured that a number of internal stakeholders were deeply engaged in the process, so that they own the outcomes and join the movement.

To unleash a firehose of ideas and get people engaged, we undertook several novel activities. We engaged with universities such as CMU in Silicon Valley, ETH in Zurich and got their students involved in hackathons and competitions to ascertain what the future of travel looked like from their vantage point. We ran internal focus groups every week, engaging a broad segment of staff from across business units. A couple of days before the focus groups met, I would issue a fictitious story, which personified the disruptions taking place. Then during the focus group, we would use the story as a backdrop to uncover the perspectives of our staff on the future. As an example, for the corporate travel focus group, we sent out the below story about Christina and her travel experience.

> Christina worked for Futureworks, a robot manufacturer out of Paolo Alto, California, specializing in making robots for the energy sector. As a senior evangelist, she was on a flight almost once every two weeks, mostly to Asia. Futureworks had recently re-hashed their corporate travel philosophy from being policy-driven to empowering their staff to take their own travel decisions, within an agreed framework. Also given the predominant Gen Z nature of their workforce, they had added some fun into an otherwise dull subject, by zoning their global travel needs into five zones and allocating points to each zone. Next week, Christina is due to fly to Sydney. This would mean a standard 10,000 points added to her travel bank for Zone 5 travel. Her cute little airline widget on her mobile had figured out that she was due to travel and notified her that she has a balance of 2000 extra points in her travel bank, thanks to some prudent usage in earlier trips. This gives her 12,000 points to pamper herself on this particular trip. Christina was amazed at how the Airline was always connected to her points system at Futureworks and gave her relevant and up-to-date information. She clicked on the 'book me' button and the Airline responded back with her preferred trip circle which would add up to 10,000 points – her business class ticket, her standard room at the Marriott, her standard red car at the airport. However, on this trip Christina wanted to relax a bit during the trip and take some time to enjoy herself. She reviewed her travel circle and saw a notification for the Vivid festival, which was running in Sydney during the her stay. Christina extended her circle by booking the event, which cost her

an additional 1200 points. That's it; she was all done and dusted in 8–10 minutes. As she stretched back in her garden, to soak in the beauty of the setting sun, she felt a sense of peace, knowing pretty well that the airline would not only take care of her, but also ensure that her company had all the relevant information to help them perform their duty of care and expense management responsibilities efficiently.

Christina's story served both as a means of communicating the art of the possible to the focus group attendees, as well as enlisting their ideas on the future of corporate travel.

We ran the first edition of our innovation summit in Dubai. Leveraging my network in tech ecosystems, we invited an eclectic mix of thought leaders who had a passion for a broad set of topics not necessarily related to travel or aviation. We intersected these thought leaders with top executives in an intimate setting over one-and-a-half days. A speaker would pitch their (often controversial) viewpoint on the topic of their passion. We would then invite interactions/ideation sessions with the company executives on how that viewpoint could help us re-imagine the future of travel. The summit was not your standard conference or executive retreat. Instead, it was an intimate and intense forum where executives could let themselves loose and intersect with competing perspectives from global thought leaders. The innovation summit's content contributed significantly to the outcomes of this stage of the process. In addition, we had a steady flow of thought leaders who would pass through Dubai on their way to the East or West. We invited them over and held sessions with multiple staff communities, thereby helping sow the seeds of change and transformation in their mindsets.

As a consequence of this approach, we were brimming with ideas from a fairly large populace, which included the university students, the hackathons, the internal focus groups, the innovation summit and our own internal staff. The next step was to summarize these ideas into a re-imagined future state for six key business domains. The format was not your traditional slideware. We built six experience stations in our Innovation Lab, which included customer and employee future journeys, minimum viable products (MVPs), and concepts that highlighted the art of the possible. We transformed the innovation lab into a re-imagined, future state of travel and aviation. In addition, we also crystalized the vision into a four-word, massively transformational purpose (MTP), along with a story that led to its unveiling.

The next step was to convert the lab into a marketplace of future-focused experiences. Every day of every week, we scheduled a set of stakeholders and pitched the vision to them in this experiential, homegrown way. Most folks murmured how inspired they felt on their way out. We also closely listened to their feedback and used it to continuously refine the experiences over the next few weeks. As a finale, we gave the same experiential update to the IT steering board members who had commissioned the initiative in the first place. They were accustomed to getting presentations in the boardroom. We of course, had no such presentation! Instead of the presentation coming to the board, we were asking the board members to go and experience the future in our lab. It was not easy, but we persisted and finally managed to get all the board members through the experiential journeys we had so passionately crafted.

If you are a disrupter, internalize the 3Ps – persistence, patience and passion. A disrupter's journey in a legacy enterprise is full of trials and tribulations. The disrupter needs a deep passion for the purpose the transformation represents, to help navigate this tumultuous journey. For example, I was convinced that our transformation will make the journeys of millions of travellers across the world easy, convenient and memorable. That was our mission and purpose, and I had a deep passion and alignment with it which helped me to stay focused and to stay the course. Another key trait of a disrupter is being persistent. On a number of occasions, like the one above with the Board, you just cannot take no for an answer and walk away. You need to get back up on your feet after each blow and find a way to get to the next milestone. And finally, as the saying goes, 'miracles happen overnight, changes take time'. Authentic disruption takes time, and you need to have the patience to see through the long journey and achieve the mission.

The end result of the vision-building step was a strong endorsement and a sense of excitement about the future state of the aviation industry that we would create by implementing the vision. The MTP also became a mantra the Board internalized, as it was so simple but profound. We received strong approval and alignment, and the internal movement had commenced. By this time, we were well into the summer months, and the entire team took a natural break for a couple of weeks.

Step three – immersion

The intuitive next step would have been to come back from the break and get straight into action – to conduct the investment planning and seek approval for the initiatives required to make the vision come alive. After all, we had strong endorsement from all key stakeholders, and conventional wisdom would suggest that we hit the investment iron when it is hot. However, I sensed that something further was required to get deeper, intrinsic commitment from our top executives. The sense and respond principle was pinging strong signals in the background. Transformation is not a short-term play. It is a long-term, deep haul. Strong intrinsic commitment at the top is key to sustain the programme and the downline investments required. While our board members were excited about the re-imagination and the art of the possible, I sensed they might still have that lingering doubt: 'Is this possible?'; 'I haven't really seen anything like this done before'; 'How will we ever go about achieving this?'

To assuage some of these potential concerns, right after the summer break, we embarked onto the next stage of action (i.e., immersion). The focus of this stage was to immerse the top of the organization and a select few executives into the world of disruption. We wanted to immerse these executives, with all their senses, into an environment where true disruption is already taking place, where the art of the possible has already become possible and where young, fresh minds are creating the future right in front of our eyes – the world of start-ups and scale-ups.

We selected three ecosystems of Silicon Valley, Berlin and London for these immersion visits. Typically, I am not a big fan of digital tourism by executives of large enterprises to tech ecosystems. However, at this stage of our journey, I sensed that immersion was necessary, and we organized a highly targeted and personalized intervention designed around our needs rather than a general visit. Getting time on diaries is never easy, but we persisted. Finally, the top two executives agreed and gave us some time for the immersion visits. Given the paucity of time at the top, we made these visits short and sharp. We needed to visit the start-ups in their homes. Sitting in those start-up hubs, in sometimes not-so-comfortable chairs, listening to the passionate co-founders describe their view of the future, how they were challenging the assumptions of a particular industry, how they planned to disrupt incumbent business models using design and advanced tech and seeing all this with our own eyes, up close and personal, was a humbling experience for all. We also experienced their ways of working – agile, nimble, flatter, fast, experimentation-led – and realized how transformation is not just about customer service or business models. It is as much about ways of working and operating models, which also need to transform to become much more agile and digitized.

We sat in an old Berlin Café, the Oberholz, with VCs and academics and learned how an entire ecosystem was fuelling and gunning for success of the disrupters. We sat in Singularity

University at Building 23, Menlo Park, and listened to their young CEO describe to us bizarre concepts such as 'mortality is a disease, and we will fix it'. We learned how exponential technologies were intersecting with each other to create new greenfield opportunities for humanity. A heated discussion followed between one of our executives and the CEO, as he brazenly rejected any doubts or pessimism around the exponential future he was describing to us. Sitting there in that dimly lit university conference room, experiencing that debate unfold, I thought this was the end of my career! The only disruption I will achieve at the end of this visit will be the one to my career and life in Dubai. However, sharp executives know when to rise well beyond the small confines of their egos. I not only retained my job, but these immersion visits very well met their intended purpose. The future we had imagined in our Lab was no longer something of distant, imaginary worlds. With the help of these immersion visits, the executives had sensed that the future was already here; it was simply not evenly distributed. Many a month later, if someone expressed doubt, you would hear them recounting one of the many stories they had experienced during these immersion visits as a counter. When we came back to base, there was a renewed confidence in our vision and our ability to achieve it.

To summarize, before you can get into the action with the Honeycomb, you need to create internal momentum behind the art of the possible. The first step is to apply force, or in other words, create a burning platform. This unsettles the inertia and clears the ground for building momentum. It would be best if you then create momentum by following a two-staged process: (1) develop a disruptive vision for the core of your business and align everyone to it through an engaging process involving both inside-out and outside-in approaches; (2) immerse your key executive stakeholders in the world of start-ups and scale-ups where disruption is already taking place. This two-staged approach worked very well in my experience to create a sustainable, nurturing ground for the execution of the disruption.

The next big question is: What do we do next? In my view, there are two strategic approaches to executing disruption in large enterprises. I call the first approach the Cube approach. In this big bang approach, we take all three dimensions of transformation, i.e., business model, operating model and technology model, and disrupt them at one go. You will need a big pot of money, big teams and a big heart, but it can be done, especially if your enterprise can allocate the big bucks for the Cube approach.

The other approach is of course the Honeycomb approach, which is inspired by both the Honeycomb and the exponential curve, the latter a common sight in world of mathematics. As described earlier, the Honeycomb framework comprises two phases that run in parallel. The disrupt phase and the capability building phase.

In the next chapter, let us dive into what these are and how they work.

02

Working the Honeycomb – disrupt phase

Disrupt is about transforming each cell within an enterprise. Disrupt it. Change it at the soul level. The cell could be a division of the enterprise or even a more atomic team. The scope is not just limited to technology. It entails a comprehensive review of all aspects of the cell's existence.

There are six nodes in any Honeycomb cell. Likewise, there are six aspects of each chosen cell of the organization which need to be reviewed and fundamentally re-hashed (see Figure 2.1). These are:

1 customer happiness

2 processes

3 ways of working

4 people

5 interfaces

6 technology or digital platforms.

Overall, the nodes of the cell represent the three key vectors of digital transformation, i.e., customer experience, operating model and culture/mindset.

Passion for customers

The customer node of the Honeycomb cell is perhaps one of the most essential ones for the Disrupt phase. The north star outcome for this

FIGURE 2.1 The Honeycomb cell

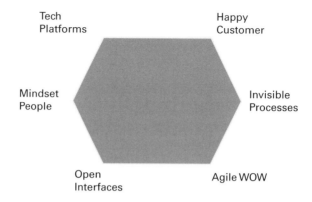

node is to create, within the cell, a deep sense of customer obsession. It does not matter whether the customers of the cell are internal or external. You cannot deliver delightful customer moments externally if internally colleagues across different cells treat each other as enemies. The cell's ethos needs to imbibe almost a fetish for the customer. In my view, in the digital era, only those paranoid about the customer survive.

In order to cook this obsessive customer recipe, a few ingredients are essential. One key ingredient is real-time data about the customer and their context. We can then use this data to hyper-personalize the engagement with customers. The best way to get this data for external customers is to offer the cell's services through digital channels/products. These products offer a digital means of customer engagement, commerce and service. I am not talking about putting up dumb web sites and/or apps. It is indeed shocking, but that is what majority of large enterprises still do. There is a big leap in shifting from running static websites to launching digital products and/or channels. Digital products can sense what the customer wants and needs while the customer is still in the journey and respond with the next best offer in real time. Digital products are characterized by the ability to run a million nano experiments each day and ultra-refine the customer's digital experience based on the outcomes and learnings from these experiments. Digital product releases are not run like marathons, but more like agile sprints, where new features are released every few weeks. The teams that create digital products are not organized by classical technology silos, but as collaborative, inter-disciplinary squads, who all work together to meet the scope, timeline and quality requirements of their assigned business missions.

Another important ingredient is changing the culture and embedding an operating model (rewards, incentives, leadership role models) which celebrates exemplary customer service. You may also need to codify a set of customer service standards and coach all the staff to use these standards. This is easier said than done, but then transformation is not for the faint hearted!

An obsession for customer service goes viral through everyday role models. They do not just speak, they act about exemplary service. When people see those actions, it shifts something intrinsically in them and they want to emulate. They share stories and narratives about these actions. I too personally encountered one such experience and it etched in my mind as a small but profound example of what authentic caring for customers actually means in real life.

I used to manage IT for the airline's operational division. The operational processes are a few strokes away from direct customer service. We used to schedule aircraft, roster crew and ensure day-to-day operational activities were in sync with the plans. As part of a technology refresh initiative, I and a dear colleague (let's call him Chris) who used to head up operations were bound for London to look at a vendor solution. The flight was in the afternoon and I was looking forward to a relaxed seven-hour journey and to be pampered by our exemplary infight services. Both Chris and I queued up at the airport services check-in desk, with Chris being in front. From the corner of my eye, I barely noticed a gentleman in front of Chris, and he was wearing a nice big hat. On the hat he seemed to have stuck a number of stickers/badges. As we approached the check-in desk, I noticed Chris suddenly step aside and get on a call. He asked me to step forward and check-in. Airline ops is a 24/7 job and I thought it must be some operations related call. Anyway, I did not think much about all this as Chris and I settled down in our seats and enjoyed a lovely journey into LHR.

The flight landed and we stepped out of the air bridge. Chris was again in front and he was greeted by one of our staff and handed a small packet. He then rushed forward and I had to sprint to catch up with him. I saw him approach that man with the hat who was ahead of us at check-in. Chris tapped him on the shoulder and said, 'I noticed you had a number of airline badges on your hat, but did not have one from our airline. Here, I arranged one for you for your collection.' With this, Chris handed him the small packet.

The astonishment and delight I saw on the man's face was priceless. No amount of corporate money can buy that memorable moment. It was a completely unexpected act of caring from an airline employee whose job description did not explicitly mention customer service. Chris was not even supposed to be working during that flight, but he had this deep passion for customer service, which resulted in this impulsive act of caring. I am sure with this simple act of surprise we had won an advocate in that customer for life.

Self-driving processes

The north star outcome for this node is to achieve autonomous business processes, imbibe adaptability and nimbleness at the core of the business, and look at opportunities to launch new business models, from re-imagined process/capabilities.

In the traditional approach, we first reviewed the process at a level of detail then re-engineered it, before applying automation to the new process. The erstwhile process for process review was (a) reengineer process, (b) optimize people effort on processes usually done through time and motion studies, (c) then apply tech.

Now we need to invert this process. First examine how the process can be completely run autonomously with artificial intelligence (AI). Can 90 per cent of your customer queries be answered by a specialist AI bot. Can all financial reconciliation be run autonomously by a reconBOT which also learns all the time from live data? Squeeze every last bit of autonomy into the business process and only then what remains can be simplified further and human ingenuity applied in the end to anything residual. This inversion will partly help achieve the mission of invisibility and velocity baked into the core of an enterprise. The other ingredient of success is to ensure that the right capabilities are applied to run this process. Ensure you have a cross-functional team, which at a minimum includes AI and process engineers, conducting the process walk throughs.

I read somewhere about an AI inspired process for decision-making. Let me share that with you. The decision framework includes three activities: (a) forecast and create a new prediction from existing data; (b) use the prediction to decide amongst options and arrive at a decision; and (c) with the decision, change some behaviours and drive new action. This action creates new data and helps refine your next decision-making process. No enterprise does this today. Perhaps it may be difficult to implement. But thinking about these new ways of thinking will get us closer to transforming the way business processes run in the digital era.

Viewing the process from an AI lens achieves two purposes. Firstly, we get bots to run most of our processes. Secondly, the process can take live input from its environment and become adaptable or achieve sentience. Baking sentience into the processes also helps the enterprise achieve nimbleness, a key requirement to thrive in the VUCA (volatility, uncertainty, complexity and ambiguity) world. Finally, as part of this process review, we should also look out for those processes which can be carved out into new business models, either organically or through a partnership with a digital native or start-up.

I personally experienced an extreme example of how a customer-facing process was ultra-personalized using advanced AI. A colleague (let us call him Sanjay) and I decided to visit Hangzhou, the home of Alibaba's HQ. Alibaba had become a shining example of a digital native rising from the East. When I gave my TEDx talk in 2018 and used Singles' Day as an example of exponential impact, Alibaba.com had earned a GMV (gross merchandise value) of $18 billion in a single 24-hour period in their Singles' Day event that year! Since then, the Singles' Day GMV has grown to $33 billion.[1] Imagine that – transacting $33 billion of revenue in 24 hours. To the linear, industrial world and mindset this kind of revenue potential is just not feasible. However, this is very much a reality in the digital world we live in today.

I remember we had some Alibaba executives in our office and we were discussing their digital platform. One of them quite humbly said, 'We are no longer just a platform, but a mini economy, as almost USD 0.5 trillion dollars of trade happens on Alibaba.com annually!' Quite fascinating. Sanjay and I decided we should get up close and personal into what makes Alibaba tick. What were some of the practices which allowed them to get this kind of exponential impact in the world?

We took a flight from Dubai to the bustling city of Shanghai. Hangzhou is a two-hour drive from Shanghai. Sanjay and I reached the beautiful city of Hangzhou in comfort, given the excellent Chinese highway infrastructure. The first thing that strikes you as you enter Hangzhou is the UNICEF World Heritage site – the West Lake.

As we walked around this historic marvel, we noticed a number of Chinese folks practicing Tai Chi in the morning and enjoying a graceful dance later in the evening. Imbibing this rustic and traditional ambience in the evening, no one could have prepared us for the complete contrast we would experience in the morning.

Next morning, a short ride from our hotel got us to the sprawling and ultra-modern Alibaba HQ. It is huge. Perhaps larger than the Google campus at Mountain View. The main building's corridors are dotted with tea and coffee facilities set among sofas and well-lit, relaxation areas. Signs remind staff to 'relax and have a cup of tea', while a large family room that resembles an airport lounge lets employees entertain their children and spend time with loved ones. Alibaba bikes are spread across the campus – pretty similar to Mountain View. All in all, the modern and digital HQ was an experience in itself. In such sharp contrast to the historic city and traditional atmosphere in and around the lake, we were in awe.

But more shock and awe was still to come. We commenced our business meetings with multiple Alibaba teams. What was clear through those conversations was that AI and data has been baked deeply into their every business process and way of working. Business executives described how the mission for big data within Alibaba was to enable data driven operations and not just personalize the digital storefront. Internal processes were also being adapted and externalized into new business opportunities. A classic example of creating new business models was how the credit score, which was created for consumers based on their interactions within the Alibaba ecosystem, later spawned into a credit agency. Then of course, the big one was their payment process system growing into Alipay.

During the course of the day, we also met their ex-Defense Advanced Research Projects Agency (DARPA) Head of Data Science. That was the most interesting and inspiring hour of our visit. We realized how advanced the platform had become in terms of adapting and personalizing the digital customer process/journey. We were informed that almost every pixel on the digital channel was customizable based on customer preferences. If a customer for instance was from Indonesia, there is a likelihood that a certain product and its image may be placed a bit more to the left on the digital store than on the right! Imagine that level of sophistication many years ago, when the rest of the world was still debating whether AI/big data were fads or transformation catalysts, whereas Alibaba was customizing its visual experience at a pixel level, based on who you were, your intent and where you came from!

Now, these new ventures born out of Alibaba's internal processes and capabilities are legendary businesses in their own right. Alipay has pivoted from being a payment provider to a marketplace of financial services products including loans, wealth management, insurance and so on. Credit scores in China are so deeply embedded that they are even used when evaluating marriage opportunities!

Agile or agile ways of working

Agile as a way of working is now quite mature, a good fit for the omni-changing digital era. If done right, agile working results in strong collaboration within the enterprise and brings along velocity.

As companies grow, they might regress significantly on the collaboration vector. Teams and individuals start competing with each other as opposed to competing with their competition. Leaders start working for their personal agendas as opposed to the purpose embodied in the enterprise they lead. Internal politics and strife eat away at the core and make the enterprise strategically weaker with every passing day. Good people resign. I often say there are two types of resignations – resigning in spirit but staying, and resigning in body and leaving. The former is much more dangerous, as typically it morphs into cynicism and angst. Mediocrity sets in.

Hence, any strategy that can positively impact internal collaboration is critical to the transformation. If you drill down into the agile principles, they are quite human-friendly and cross-applicable to multiple business domains. My top three agile principles are:

- A sharp focus on human interactions and collaboration, and not just romance with processes and tools. The larger the enterprises and longer their lifespan, the greater the reliance on processes as a means of getting work done. Agile guides you to make the processes just right, to make the human co-operation more prominent. To organize multi-disciplinary teams, give them a mission, set a supportive environment and you will experience them collaborate and deliver outcomes together.

- To embrace change and not just romance with the plan. Plan, command and control was a pattern fit for the industrial era. Now we need to sense the environment continuously and then respond. Agile guides you to show deep affection toward change and embrace it – to become antifragile. Agile guides you to shift to a paradigm where you actually look forward to and thrive in the wake of continuous, relentless change.

- To break down work into autonomous small blocks and dial up the cadence. Agile guides you to conduct daily stand-ups. It helps everyone get together. It helps to dial up the velocity of the operating culture – to conduct periodic retrospectives. It helps everyone bond and celebrate, to practise iteration planning. It helps break down work into manageable chunks. It helps everyone collaborate and think about the future. I am not recommending that you follow the entire nine yards of the agile framework. However, if you just follow two to three such practices and processes, you will experience agility creep into your ways of working and dial up the speed of delivery.

In my early days of creating momentum for agile methods within a large enterprise, I hired a scrum master who was from Australia. He was excellent – someone who embraced the business mission, did not fall into the classical trap of seeing himself as an order-taker, but as an equal partner to the business colleagues in the transformation journey.

I distinctly remember one of his comments in a steering group of senior corporate executives. This was during the early days of the agile project. On being prompted, he said something to this effect: 'For the ongoing sprint and the next one, you have no decision rights. There is nothing that can be changed. The train has left. A release time has been set and will be met. The prior agreed features will be delivered as promised. However, for the subsequent sprints, you have complete flexibility and decision rights. When I groom the requirements with your teams, they are fully empowered to change whatever they want.'

Imagine going to the top echelons of a traditional enterprise and saying you have no decision rights! Some may consider this extreme, but I strongly believe his message was spot on. Time is considered a commodity in large enterprises. But in the digital era, velocity is a competitive weapon. We need to able to break down work into smaller chunks, clearly agree outcomes for each sprint (which is typically a piece of work delivered within a two-to-three-week time, and then ensure work for upcoming sprints is not disturbed by executive procrastination or politics. Decisions taken need to be honoured and executed, and since each sprint decision has a smaller scope, it is not like you are putting the enterprise at risk. The release train concept of agreeing a set of dates when work will be delivered is a powerful change lever. The positive result of this concept is that you get tangible business outcomes every few weeks with a new release going to production and being put to use. The other, diametrically opposite concept is that for future sprints you can pretty much change what-ever you want. This provides the flexibility and agility to sense the environment and respond in real time. This helps the organization become much nimbler in its operating model.

In another setting, we had completed the 'momentum building' for transformation within a large enterprise. The massively transforma-tion purpose (MTP) had been crafted and internalized. Top line transformational storyline for the core of the business had also been envisioned. The next step was to look at each critical area of the busi-ness and develop its future state, along with the capabilities/investment required to achieve that future state.

The first area was the business model itself and what exactly it should transform into. In addition, and in parallel, we were also creating the future state of the operating model including core processes such as distribution, pricing, inventory management, supplier ecosystems, etc. Given our strong passion for agile, we ran this programme using agile principles. It was brilliant to collate a set of cross-functional teams to work on creating the future of the enterprise. The teams were truly multi-disciplinary and, as a first, we also included our partners and supplier team members into these teams.

Initially, there was the usual resistance from all business managers. How can I release my best people to work on this activity? We have a business to run here! However, we persisted and initially set up the teams with whoever we could muster. Then, as per the delivery orientation, outcomes started coming out from these teams on a two-weekly cadence. These outcomes were widely shared and celebrated within the enterprise. This created excitement at all levels with the organization. And as expected, those managers who resisted developed fear of missing out (FOMO) and, in the next iterations, started themselves releasing their resources to the sprint teams. Eventually, the programme scaled nicely and was also very balanced in its distribution of resources and capabilities. More importantly, the act of working together in these teams built a level of grass-root bond between diverse organizational silos, and when members were rotated out into their regular jobs, the bonhomie and collaboration were retained. This to me is an even more important outcome of the agile method. It promotes a sense of collaboration and togetherness within an enterprise, which can serve as a significant competitive advantage for the existing business model as well as a great enabler for the transformation journey. The small 'a' in agile is perhaps the more important aspect; however, some of the methods of the big 'A' in Agile framework can definitely be deployed across the enterprise to achieve organization-wide agility.

Mindset and people

Know to learn rather than learn to know. Be open to co-creation. Show love for change and ambiguity. Foster an environment and mindset where capability eats credentials for lunch, where hierarchies are built into the network, where power is curiosity, where sharing is the new caring, and where leaders follow and serve.

These are the north star principles of the digital mindset. This is a critically important node of the Honeycomb. I strongly believe, given the sensitivity and criticality of the people bit, this process of renewal needs to be done first and fast. And, as is inherent with this approach, we do not start by changing the mindset of the whole big enterprise. We start one cell at a time. There is also a harsh reality to this aspect of the transformation. It impacts people. The enterprise does not have a mindset. It is the people within the enterprise whose mindset needs to change – sometimes, people who have been in the enterprise for several decades. Over the years, having done it multiple times across organizations, I suggest the following process to refresh and renew the people workforce within each cell, so that they are much more aligned with the digital mindset.

Let us call this people transformation exercise the Honeycomb phoenix process. The phoenix is a mystical bird which rose from the ashes and is a symbol of rebirth and renewal. Given the need for a deep renewal of the people capability and associated mindset within an enterprise, phoenix is an apt name for this process.

Mindset transformation must start at the top, as culture in most organizations is set there. Hence, phoenix concentrates on reviewing and refreshing the top three leadership levels in any given cell. The process has the following regimented steps:

- Firstly, there must be a strategic context to the transformation. This is the new digital strategy or the new digital transformation strategy, which is the reason why this process is being run. Not detailed in reems of paper, but just a simple picture which clarifies 'what' digital transformation means to the enterprise. Well before phoenix can begin, you need to create this digital strategy, ensure this is clearly endorsed at the board level and shared with all the chiefs or executive officers (CxOs) of the enterprise.

- While the strategy is set at the enterprise level, the new operating model is set at the cell level. This is again at a fairly high level. It clarifies how the enterprise's digital strategy will impact the cell's operating model. The operating model typically comprises the core business processes of the cell.

- Only when the new digital strategy and operating model have been defined and communicated can you then start creating a new functional structure for the cell. Also given these changes, the existing organization structure becomes defunct. The functional structure is translated in a new organizational structure up to x-3 level for the cell. All job descriptions for these leadership roles are re-written over a time-boxed 3–4-day period.

The above steps are co-created closely with human resources (HR). In fact, the talent transformation is a co-owned initiative by the chief data officer (CDO)/chief technology officer (CTO) and chief human resources officer (CHRO). So in the phoenix process, digital strategy is created, followed by a new operating model in alignment with the strategy, followed by functional structure, followed by a new org structure. Only after all this pre-work is professionally done, at speed, do you get into the people stream.

The people stream is carried out over a maximum 7–10-day period, including the weekend. It follows the below strict flow of events:

- Two days before the weekend, all impacted staff (x-1, x-2, x-3) are called into a phoenix event. This is a time-boxed, one-hour event. The chief human resources officer and chief data officer/chief technology officer give a presentation on the context (strategy, operating model, new org structure) and the Phoenix Project Manager informs the impacted staff about the next steps.

- All staff are invited to give expressions of interest (EOI) for all new leadership roles within the cell's new organization structure. Each staff member can only submit a maximum of two EOIs. Each staff can only apply for one role higher that their current role. For example, x-3 can apply to only one x-2 or x-1 role, and the second EOI must be for an x-3 role. They can choose to use both EOIs for roles at their current level.

- An electronic channel is then opened for communications as well as receiving the EOIs over two working days plus the weekend.

Typically, by noon on the first working day next week, the EOI process closes out.

- A composite, C-Level panel is set up for the interview process.
- A set of three to four case studies are sent out over the weekend to all the impacted staff. They should choose one and present their views on it.
- The panel allows 20 minutes for presentation on the case study, followed by 40 minutes of Q&A by the C-level panellists.
- The panellists are coached on the mindset attributes we are looking for. Through a delphi method, senior executives then take decisions on the applicants' fit. The delphi method uses the collective wisdom of the experts involved to take a decision. Either they are fit to the role applied, fit to a lower level or different role, or do not fit at all.

All decisions are time-boxed, and all new appointments are decided and announced within the 7–10-day window. Ad interim appointments are made for all roles where no internal candidates have been found.

All exits are dealt with swiftly.

An away day is organized for the new cell's leadership within a couple of weeks of appointment, where they bond with each other and start working together on implementing the new digital strategy.

Typically, I have observed the following patterns through this process:

- Those chief executive officers (CxOs) who come into the process with their natural bias towards incumbent candidates quickly loose this bias through deep involvement with the process. The process takes over and they end up taking decisions one would have never imagined they would take at the start.
- Some junior employees emerge as the surprise package. I have run five of these phoenix processes and this is always the case. People with a great mindset may have been subdued under the weight of hierarchy. They rise and are unanimously appointed by the senior panel.

- Staff who are misfit from a mindset perspective mostly make it to the exit list. Like with any selection process, you never get a 100 per cent success rate and some employees may still make it through the process without having the right mindset.

- While there is deep involvement of the executives in the process, invariably when some of their favourites do not make it, expect some escalation or the other by the CxOs, especially at the start of the process.

- At the end, even the strongest distractors and cynics – those whom you had to include in the process kicking and screaming – will eventually admit that the process worked well and that they are reluctantly happy with it!

There is a strong correlation between organizational mindset and its people. Hence, people transformation is an important step in this journey. As long as the process is executed in an equitable and fair manner, and done quickly, it sets up the cell for the larger transformation ahead. The folks who remain feel invigorated and charged up to make a difference. The key ingredient of success is the strict and fast-paced timetable of this process. In my experience, the scope can be changed a bit; however, given the sensitivity of this exercise, the deadlines need to be announced at the start and strictly met.

Mindset and storytelling

Like customer service, mindset can be unearthed and propagated more through stories and narratives as opposed to reports and KPIs. I experienced an interesting story which highlights how the digital natives have shaped their mindset around talent acquisition and retention. This relates to one of the GAFA (Google, Amazon, Facebook, Apple) companies, who have been born digital and then scaled digitally. I was in Berlin. We stayed at the Hotel Adlon Kempinski – an absolute marvel – and around it there was history in all its glory. Since I had visited East Berlin in my childhood when the Berlin Wall was still intact, this was a very special trip for me – to experience the transformation of the city from those days of division and rife.

Equally interesting was the vibrancy of the tech ecosystem in Berlin. It has all the ingredients of Silicon Valley (universities, start-ups, venture capitals, events... perhaps not the weather) but at a much smaller scale. I particularly enjoyed the design focus of the ecosystem as well as the inflow of talent from Eastern Europe, who had made Berlin their home. In between visiting the start-ups, I took a break to visit the AI centre for one of the GAFA companies. I was intrigued by the fact that the American company would set up its AI centre in Berlin. Firstly, so far away from base and secondly, it was not as if Berlin had some special AI and math talent. I met the head of the AI centre and it was quite impressive to hear what they were doing there. But this question kept nagging me through his presentation. So, towards the end, I popped it out: why would this US behemoth set up an AI centre in Berlin of all the places in the world? His answer stumped me. He said, quite nonchalantly, 'Well, that is quite simple. They wanted to recruit me. I told them clearly that I prefer to be in Berlin. So, they said, "OK, go there and build your centre!"'

Though my initial reaction was that of surprise, when I reflected on this conversation a bit later, I realized that there was a profound lesson in it for traditional companies and mindsets. Large, branded enterprises have been used to talent lining up at their doors for decades. However, in today's digital era, for some special digital skills or mindsets, we have to be where the talent is and not vice versa. Now I agree, this is not relevant for all skills. However, the very fact that digital natives – even those which have become so famous and can attract anyone – shed their egos for special talent and find novel ways of enticing them to join was a great lesson on the humility required to operate in the digital era. It is a humbling lesson for all large enterprise line managers and their HR brethren. When you get the right mindset and skillset, take care of them so that they can take care of your transformation.

Renewing your people capability within each cell through a structured and fast paced process such as phoenix, with a view to build and embed a digital mindset, will go a long way in powering the transformation effort.

Open interfaces/gateways

Gateways are a historical capability. Cities and countries built them to invite people and trade onto their shores. The digital world is no different. Larger enterprises need to build convenient gateways for the outside world to connect with them – not only to use their services, but to build new business models over the services. These services manifest themselves as application programming interface (API) gateways. The world can use the APIs to consume the services the enterprise provides. But perhaps more importantly, the technology experts can use these APIs to spawn new digital businesses using your services. This converts your business from a pipeline to a platform business model. Use each cell's transformation journey to create APIs for the key business services offered by the cell. Ensure these APIs are nicely hosted into a centralized, enterprise wise API gateway. The cumulation of business services, easily accessible by the external world through standardized APIs, is key to unleashing the move toward exponential business models.

In a start-up, teams are small and almost everyone has clear line of sight to the customer. They work together and though there clearly are individual expertise areas such as sales, marketing, product and so on, they all work as one team in service of the customer. As companies scale, inevitably the teams also grow. This results in larger teams managing those expertise areas. That per se is not an issue; however, large teams working in expert domains also bring along a very dangerous legacy construct – the organization 'silo'. This term is almost non-existent in the start-up lingo, yet so very predominant in large enterprise parlance. So much value seeps through the crevices of these organizational silos. Not many people directly relate the value loss to these crevices. But in my experience, this is definitely one of the predominant root causes.

As part of this node of the Honeycomb, our job is to build strong, open, and transparent bridges across these enterprise expertise areas so that the negative effect of silos can be mitigated. These bridges come in the form of services as described earlier, which each cell should expose so that that the world outside the cell can consume it.

In some cases, the services will be directly exposed to the customer. In some cases, the services will be exposed to an internal customer. In both cases, the same level of passion is required to create a clean, transparent and open interface layer to the cell's services and experiences. In some cases, the cell can expose its services digitally, in the form of standard APIs, and give a boost to the API economy. In some other cases, the cell may not have any digital interfaces, as the service provided requires a human interface and touch. Even in this case, it is important to provide a clear and clean information layer of the human services being provided and ensure the human layer is trained to provide the interface in a consistent manner.

Besides the impact on organizational silos, open interfaces at each cell level also help the organization become nimbler and build entirely new business models. Adaptability is the ability of the organization to change course fast, based on internal or external unplanned events. With each cell clearly exposing its services, the organization can re-configure itself quickly by assimilating services in response to any external event. Large enterprises have a competitive advantage in terms of their customer base, distribution, infrastructure, intellectual property, etc. However, traditionally these capabilities can only be orchestrated together. You either get the entire enterprise as a whole or nothing. However, deconstructing a large enterprise into cells, with their interfaces cleanly exposed as a set of services, allows the enterprise to mix its internal capabilities with external innovators such as start-ups or digital natives and launch new business models.

Look at what is going on in the banking sphere. Fintechs are attacking every aspect of the banking world. Some banks are doing nothing, burying their head in the sand and praying this passes. Some others have re-imagined themselves as a set of core internal capabilities. They are exposing these capabilities as a set of services – called banking as a service (BAAS) – to the outside world and inviting the start-up world to build partnerships with them. This is a classic case of how open interfaces can be leveraged to foray into new digital business models.

Tech

And finally, there is the tech. Do not be shy of recognizing its importance. Do not just fall for the cliché 'transformation is not about the tech'. Though I agree that it is not the whole of the transformation, tech is quite an important ingredient in the digital soup. Just because you don't understand it, or even worse don't want to, does not mean someone is not going to use it to commoditize your business model. A first step is to stop evangelizing tech as a specialist skill. In the digital era, tech is a critical competence. Everyone needs to embrace and imbibe it. I am not talking about learning to write code or configure servers. It is the ability to understand tech just enough to develop strategic foresight about its potential.

The tech world is going through a transformation of its own. There is so much invention. There is so much change. There is such a pace. It is so beautiful. All layers of the tech stack are in a state of constant change. Infrastructure now resides in the cloud. If you still run your cell digitally on-premises, just shift. Do not think, just do it. Manage exceptions as an exception. Do not make them the rule. The other transformative tech has been AI. AI as a technology has had so many winters through the years. The term AI was coined in 1956 – can you believe it?! For a number of years, it ordained the world of research and movies. However, now it is hitting prime time, in both the consumer as well as the enterprise worlds. For me, the tipping point in AI came when Lee Sedol was defeated in a game of Go and in the story of Move 37.

Go is a 3000-year-old game. The creator was perhaps an alien, but most definitely an absolute genius. Emperors Yao and Shun garner equal votes as the creator of Go among historians. The creation went viral. Over 14 million people play it today, mostly in Asia – a mysterious gift from mythical China. Unlike chess or checkers, which have a large but still manageable number of moves, a Go game has over 10^{170} possible moves – more than the number of atoms in the universe. Definitely beyond the capabilities of a brute force calculation. When maestros recount their wins in a Go game, they often use words such as 'intuition' and 'inspiration'. So, you cannot calculate your way to a win in Go. This is unlike games like chess, wherein powerful computers can use brute force to calculate all possible moves at each stage of the game and beat grand masters using computing power. In sharp contrast, Go is (mostly) won and lost on one of the most exotic human qualities of intuition. You cannot model human intuition into a mathematical equation.

In the recorded history of Go, players describe iconic moves which completely turned a game on its head. Truly inspired and original moves. Singular moves that a player will play only once in a lifetime. Such moves have been aptly referred to as 'divine moves'. Conventional wisdom says that you cannot just brute force your way into becoming intuitive or divine.

March 2016 was an iconic milestone in the evolution of AI. AlphaGo, an AI Go algorithm created by the UK-based and Google-acquired DeepMind, challenged the Roger Federer of Go, grand-master Lee Sedol, to a tournament of five games. It was one of the most watched and anticipated events in Asia, with the excitement most palpable in South Korea, where this unique contest was held. Top Google executives added to the buzz by descending on Korea to watch the contest. Pundits predicted an easy win and a clean sweep by Lee Sedol. Lee is a national hero. The most creative, unconventional, inspired player in the world. Top dog. There was no way a mere equation was going to beat billions of years of evolutionary contribution to human intuition and inspiration…

AlphaGo beat Lee four games to one.

The world watched in shock and awe. History in the making. And if that was not enough, AlphaGo played a completely inspired move in the second game. This was Move 37. The move was so obscure, unconventional and unexpected that it sent Lee Sedol into a spin. He actually got off his chair and disappeared for 15 minutes. A divine move, played by a computer running an equation! After the game, when DeepMind's scientist examined the flight recorder of the second game, they learnt that the probability given to AlphaGo for making that move was 1 in 10,000. Despite the odds, AlphaGo still decided to play Move 37 and surprised its opponent out of the game.

The story, however, does not end there. For me, this last part is perhaps the most important bit. In the fourth game, Lee Sedol played the much-famed Move 78. It was a divine move from Lee – a completely unconventional, inspired manoeuvre. The next level of human inspiration. It sent AlphaGo into a tailspin. The AI lost its bearings and lost the game quickly thereafter.

What a story this is. An AI beat the top dog, human genius 4–1 in perhaps the world's most complex game, a game which can only be won using the most human attributes of intuition and inspiration. To top it all, the AI also played a divine move, to add to the intrigue. But then the human, learning quickly from his digital twin, came back strongly with the next level of inspiration, surprising himself as well as the equation.

In this story lies many an inspiration and learning opportunity. To those with heads buried in the sand, AI is here to stay, to transform, to exponentially impact the world of business and societies. It is not a fad; it is not a passing cloud which will disappear by the time you retract from the darkness of the sand. It may not be human or divine yet, but it is not just a dumb equation either. It is at the cusp of an inflection point. It is getting ready to have an unprecedented impact on humanity. Those who will welcome it with a loving embrace will leapfrog exponentially to a blue ocean of differentiation. The impact will be limited only by the extent of human imagination. And as we delegate more work and get challenged by our AI digital twins, we will ourselves transcend to a new level of cognitive capability, as Lee did with Move 78. That for me is the AI mantra. AI is augmented intelligence, assisting us in managing cognitive tasks, assisting us to rise toward new levels of intelligence, augmenting us in all spheres of life.

This tipping point in the advancement of AI strengthens my belief of AI being a critical foundation for the transformation. Enterprises need to pay heed and invest in AI for every cell of the Honeycomb. A key ingredient for success of any AI is, however, data. Hence enterprises need to collect as much data about the cell in real time. The world moves fast nowadays. Turn up the cadence of your data flows to real time from the very start. The incremental effort is not material from batch to real time. It is just about using the right tools. Also, do not worry if you cannot for now think about the use of a particular data set. Collect it and clean it, nevertheless. Data has an options value. Do not worry too much about people telling you that you will end up creating a data swamp. Those are the people shouting out loud from the industrial era. Those who are operating in the digital era do not think about such arguments. They are collecting data like there is no tomorrow and then using advanced data science on the data to leapfrog the world. So, start this mission with each cell. Make every cell big and fast data enabled.

AI is not the only exponential technology, though. There are numerous others. And that is the differentiating characteristic of the digital era we live in. There are so many technologies impacting us left, right and centre that it is sometimes difficult to keep up. Blockchain, quantum, nano tech, genetics, you name it! Each of them is moving at pace, and also intersections between them are producing interesting possibilities. Blockchain has gone through many winters, like AI when it comes to the enterprise context. Lately, however, permissioned business networks have become a stable pattern to deliver business value in ecosystems as varied as food, supply chain, finance, shipping, etc.

I had the good fortune of seeing a quantum computer in IBM's research centre in Zurich. Hanging inside one of their rooms was the quantum computer. It looked like a hot water geyser found in most Indian households! A few years back, I would hear about quantum only from large companies such as IBM, Google and so on. However, in late 2019 at an event in Silicon Valley, three start-ups presented their companies based on quantum. When start-ups start digging into a technology, it usually means that an explosion of activity is not far away. I am quite excited about the possibilities with quantum.

It is so important for enterprises to keep tab on these technology trends. It is not good enough to think of IT as a support function which asks, 'how high?' each time you ask it to jump. Enterprise executives need to understand the strategic impact these technologies are having on their business already and get ready to react or leverage them to leapfrog competition in the future.

There is another aspect of legacy enterprises which is usually buried in legacy – its application estate. It is critical that we reform the tech applications of each cell. Applications are the only layer which faces off with the people. We cannot leave that interface in the legacy world and expect a transformation. There are two options for us to reform the application estate in legacy enterprises. The first is to stop putting lipstick on the pig and do a complete re-write. This is a good option for certain applications. The re-write itself can be done choosing one of three predominant patterns: (1) write code and create ground up; (2) choose a predominant module and build/assemble around it; or (3) assemble using a number of readily available micro-services running on the cloud and only code those which you can't find. I recommend the third pattern.

The second option for application estate reform is to leave the 'systems of record' as-is and concentrate your effort on the systems of engagement which face off with your customers as well as systems of intelligence which provide the differentiating capability. You can 'hollow the core' of some of the applications which hold the system of record by slowly peeling off modules into new era application architectures. The one problem with this option is that the core remains the same and you will hit some or other issue with the legacy core, which will adversely impact your disruptive ambitions.

Conclusion

This then is the disrupt phase with the six nodes of the Honeycomb. Six mini-missions per enterprise cell, resulting in the comprehensive, DNA level overhaul of the cell. If done right, the disrupt phase will result in customer obsession being baked into the soul of the cell and its processes powered by AI and data transforming to being self-driving or invisible. The ways of working will become agile, driving velocity and nimbleness. A new digital mindset will take shape, initiated by a structured process to renew the people capability. New tech architectures, so common in the consumer world, will be welcomed and leveraged in the enterprise – tech that is intuitive and data enabled and for which adoption is not a change management initiative. Adoption just happens. Intuitively. Organically.

When you look back at this new cell, which has gone through the six nodes of the Honeycomb approach, you will notice a butterfly emerge gently.

Endnote

1 Tinker, M (2017) 'Alibaba's $33b Singles Day rides China's third wave of development', *Financial Review*, 12 November. www.afr.com/markets/alibabas-33b-singles-day-rides-chinas-third-wave-of-development-20171112-gzjoi8 (archived at https://perma.cc/BM7A-2HAF)

03

Working the Honeycomb – digital capabilities

If you continue to disrupt each Honeycomb cell in an isolated way, you will get amazing results, no doubt. But these isolated disruptions will not yield the sudden exponential upsurge for your organization as a whole. Something more is required to get to that tipping point, beyond which there is a steep surge of the enterprise toward the exponential zone – beyond which the sum of the parts is an exponential whole, beyond which lies the much coveted true and meaningful digital disruption of the entire enterprise. This something is about building a strong foundation of digital capabilities, which act as the nurturing ground on which disruption can blossom.

Each cell's disruption journey needs to be connected to a set of foundational digital era enterprise capabilities. While the scope of the disrupt stage of Honeycomb approach is limited to each cell, the capabilities have an enterprise-wide scope. Inspired by the Honeycomb pattern, there are six enterprise capabilities which need to be built and nurtured as part of the Honeycomb approach. Let us explore these digital capabilities.

Data and AI (DNA)

This is perhaps one of the most important enterprise capabilities. There are so many clichés around data: that it is the new oil; that it is a new asset class; 'In God we trust, everyone else bring data'. And guess what, all of these are true. Data is enormously important in this journey. It is critical that as you transform each cell, we connect the part data from the cell into a whole for the enterprise. And this is done in real time. The technical architecture for this connectivity has been sorted out. No need to re-invent or re-imagine this piece. Just build a data lake using one of the many cloud-native technologies. Stream each cell's data into the lake, in real time. Ensure all atomic data is stored in the lake, then model it to create your enterprise golden records. I typically call these the genomes: the customer genome; the location genome; the product genome. Ensure the technical architecture of the genomes is such that they can grow horizontally infinitely, i.e., have as many attributes as you can have. Also grow vertically infinitely, i.e., you can have as many of them as you like. Then ensure you have created a serving layer over the genome layer, so as to democratize the power of these genomes across your enterprise. Anyone should be able to use the evolving knowledge in these genomes across your enterprise. In addition, ensure that on top of your data lake you have built the ability to conduct machine learning and AI work; that is the primary reason for building the lake in the first place. As each cell feeds more and more data into your lake, the analytical potential for your enterprise will grow with it. You will be able to discover unique insights and wisdom from advanced machine learning (ML)/AI algorithms. This wisdom will help as a differentiator to compete. To provide ultra-personalized experience to your customers. Not just to automate your processes, but to run your enterprise autonomously.

Centralize or decentralize?

There is a lot of debate within organizations on whether to centralize or decentralize the data and analytics capability. Some set up centralized centres of excellence (COE) for data and analytics and give them end-to-end charge of collating organizational data as well as performing analytics on topic of the collated data. Some prefer to federate out the capability to different departments within the organization. There are pros and cons of both approaches. However, I am a strong proponent of a federated set-up and architecture for data and analytics. There may be a case to collate sparse talent into a centre of excellence initially, but the eventual goal should be to federate this strategic capability. Analytical acumen, built on good quality, real-time data, is critical to thrive in the digital era we all live in. Hence, it is an imperative for every role to build and hone this analytical ability. We may need a central body to set and operate the governance framework for data; however, the analytical execution should happen close to the business and where the data is produced.

In terms of talent, this is one of the hardest to find and retain talent pools. I suggest building a small but strong kernel team of data, analytics and AI professionals and then the remaining talent can be sourced from partners. Once the kernel team has been established, one can also source fresh university students and mould them into these critical roles. While there are a number of fancy roles associated with this discipline, I believe one of the most important ones relates to ensuring we get clean data across the enterprise. This janitorial work over enterprise data is critical. Most enterprises struggle with this bit and then wonder why their COEs did not offer any noticeable transformation or outcome. As the cliché goes, 'garbage in, garbage out'. If we do not sort out the quality of data and resolve inherent conflicts relating to data definitions, there is no chance, deeper in the analytical pipeline, to derive significant value from all the data and analytics effort. Hence, please ensure you hire some top data janitors and give them the organizational freedom to clean up your enterprise data, before you begin any sophisticated work such as writing AI use cases.

Co-create

This is both a capability and a mindset. It is the ability to join up two or more talent pools towards achieving a collective mission. It is also a mindset which stays humble and recognizes that not all answers are available within. The advent of the internet has made it possible for co-creative activity to span distant, geographically spread teams. Anyone can assemble individuals or experts across the world and assign them tasks. All you need is the will to do so. The mechanism is just a click away.

One of the best examples which brought the concept and potential of co-creation to life for me relates to my daughter's urge to write a poetry book when she was a teenager. I had just returned from the office and went to my daughter's room. She was hugely excited about something. On asking, I was informed rather enthusiastically that she had written poetry for the first time. There were eight poems and each one took inspiration from some food item, such as coffee or chocolate. I was quite excited that my daughter had intersected the world of poems and art with the world of food. I strongly believe that most innovation rests in the creative intersection of two unrelated disciplines. Hence, I was happy to see my daughter invoke such an intersection without prompting. Having created her seminal piece, she of course wanted to share it with her friends. I promised to create some prints for her and that was that.

However, that night, I kept thinking about this capability of co-create and how my response to my daughter had been so traditional, without using any of the capabilities of the digital world we live in. So, I got up in the middle of the night and kicked-in co-create in earnest. I first registered myself into a platform which democratizes work called Upwork.com. I wanted to intersect some artwork into my daughter's eight poems. Hence, I launched a global task for creating art for each of the eight poems my daughter had created. Fourteen artists responded from across the world in around 10 hours' time. When I got up in the morning, I had 14 costed proposals! I selected a young girl who had not earned anything yet on Upwork and gave her the job digitally. Within around 72 hours she had turned around the eight pieces of art and after a few iterations I gave the final approval and paid using my digital wallet.

Now I had eight beautiful poems in the intersection of poetry and food and eight lovely pieces of artwork, created by someone sitting on a different continent, all at lower double-digit USD expenditure. I used a digital software to assemble the artwork into the poem and then created a final version of my daughter's beautiful poem book. As a final leg of this co-creative journey, I used a couple of online publishing platforms to publish the poem book and used content and marketing platforms such as Facebook to share with friends and make them aware of the book's existence. You can imagine the glow on my daughter's face when she experienced the final product both in print form as well as digitally available to a global audience. A face resplendent in the reflection of the co-creative effort which had underpinned the poem book's creation.

This is the beautiful world we live in today – where a young teenager, sitting in her bedroom in the Middle East, can assemble the power of a global talent pool and co-create something brand new from scratch and then make it available for the world to consume. This is the power of co-creation.

We need to design our enterprises and work activities with co-create in mind. We need to hire people who are able to work in this new paradigm. For example, in my young age when we used to interview for coders, we would give them a business requirement and then ask them, 'What would you do with this now?' And of course, the correct answer then was, 'Well, I will take the requirement, design it and then I will code it'. After all, we were interviewing a coder and one would expect the right answer is that a coder would code. However, in today's co-creative paradigm I will not hire a coder who answers this way. The right answer is that, before they start coding, they should look in the vast repositories of open-source code or APIs that exist in the world to see if they can assemble, re-use an already created piece of code and only extend the same for their particular use case. They should co-create their piece of code with someone else's already existing one. That is how we get speed and impetus and rapid innovation in today's world. Hence this co-create capability is a must for enabling the transformation.

Communities of passion

In my experience, this is the nucleus of any change. A community of talent. A pool of multipliers. A carefully chosen coterie of catalysts. Those who can ignite intrigue. Those who can rub off their passion onto others. Those who are antifragile and thrive in continuous change. And above all, those who are storytellers, able to convert success stories from the cell's transformation into enterprise folklore.

Identify these talent gems as you rummage through each cell's transformation, then arrange them into a virtual community. Pepper them with regular engagement and digital work. This team will infuse and fuel the spirit of transformation in your entire enterprise.

I had the good fortune of experiencing a community of passion in action within a large enterprise. It was the very early days of the launch of apps. The iPhone and the Apple app store had just been invented. While the consumer world was downloading apps to their mobiles, the enterprise world was still looking up from desktops. I was running the innovation lab in a large enterprise and we could see on the horizon that consumption of business services from a mobile device was imminent. But of course, the capabilities to deliver these mobile services did not exist, neither did we have any funding in those early days for mobile enabling the services. So, we set out to experiment with the community concept.

We were fortunate to have a captive software engineering base in-house. One late evening, we held an event with the software engineers to launch the Spring community. The concept was simple. We invited our engineers to contribute their time to building apps for staff. We invited staff to contribute ideas and features that would make their life easy when available on their mobiles. The innovation lab provided the base platform where this community of engineers and staff could collaborate and interact. It was a non-traditional attempt to usher in a new capability into the enterprise. What happened next was fascinating. Driven by their passion to learn this new technology (app development), the engineers swamped the community. Very soon they started producing cool internal apps, which added direct value to our staff. We made those apps easily available through an enterprise app store, which we called Spring. As more and more staff used these internal apps, they too got excited and contributed more ideas into the Spring platform. It was network effect in action. All we did was to nurture the community and very soon it became a foundational capability for internal mobile app development. For the staff, by the staff, orchestrated and nurtured by staff – a value-adding community, driven by passion for the greater good. Over the years, we have had flight attendants spend time during their rostered leave to do graphic designs for certain apps. We had flight captains contribute code during their time off. The community evolved well beyond mobile development into any new technology which was rising in the horizon. We have mini communities for AI, blockchain and other such tech advances where an initial period of experimentation was required before it could be scaled.

Although this story is tech focused, communities of passion need to be developed across multiple capabilities and are a key pillar for the transformation. They help create a bridge between learning by disrupting each cell into the enterprise's people capability, which can then be redeployed in disrupting the next cell. In addition, it enables the multiplier effect, which is critical for scaling the disruption across the entire enterprise.

Academy

When you look at the rear view of your enterprise's talent pool, or in fact when you look at any other aspect of your enterprise, you should see two distinct views: legacy and heritage. I have seen too many new executives come into legacy incumbents and have their eyesight tinted with only one view, i.e., legacy. That is all they see. Everything is broken. There is no good in the historical good performance of the company. I have come from the outside, you are all broken, I know what to do and I am going to fix it! Well, that does not work. Every large enterprise has both legacy and heritage embedded in their assets. This holds especially true for talent. The art of talent management in the digital age is having the serenity to accept the heritage, courage to change the legacy and having the wisdom to know the difference.

You need to kit-up internal talent for the digital era. The war for talent is fierce. You are not suddenly going to be able to hire externally for all critical roles. And even if you were such an attractive employer, you definitely want a good intersection of internal and external talent to lead you through this transformation journey.

In order to build a strong internal capability for disruption, a new age learning environment is required – a new age academy. The purpose of the academy should be to build internal disrupters. The learning journey of a disrupter goes through three phases: the inspire phase, where the disrupter wakes up to the 'art of the possible'; the immerse phase, where the disrupter immerses in the real-world of disruption, not through PowerPoint slides, but through a deep 'touch and feel' immersion into this new world; and the do phase, wherein the disrupter takes charge of a small area of the business, a Honeycomb cell, and actually disrupts its six nodes. In doing so, they acquire real-life experience of disruption with all its trials and tribulations. The academy is a critical enterprise-wide digital capability. It aims to increase the surface area of your digital leadership. It acts as a breeding ground for disrupters.

Perceptual acuity

My very first hackathon was in the heart of Silicon Valley. My team and I were enlisting outside-in ideas on the future of travel. The duration of the hackathon was 24 hours. By late in the evening, the registrations started filling up and then grew exponentially – so much so that we had to regrettably deny entry to a few teams from top institutes. The physical event space had run out, so we had no other choice but to refuse a few aspiring hackers. Nevertheless, when I looked around the buzzing hall later in the night, I saw a room full of participants from all walks of life, with laptops in their hands, raring to go. After my initial speech to welcome them and set the context of the challenge, the teams started to work their magic. I did not know what to expect. It was exciting to see all these strangers working with such passion and commitment on a challenge defined by us.

Despite the buzz, I was sceptical of the value we would derive from the event. Anyway, the hackathon ran its course for the next 24 hours and at the end we set up a marketplace where each team presented their outcome to a judging panel. As I toured the market-place, I was pleasantly surprised. The true meaning of 'wisdom of the crowds' dawned on me. The ideas presented and displayed by the hackers in the travel domain were well beyond my imagination. There was no way, despite my several years of industry experience, I could have given birth to so many novel and innovative ideas! No way.

This outside-in approach to innovation and building a global innovation ecosystem capability will propel your transformation. I am not talking about periodic digital tourism to Silicon Valley by your execs. We need a much more immersive and involved innovation capability. The ecosystem should include relationships with academia, start-ups, thought leaders, disrupters. I earlier described the annual Innovation Summit, wherein we would assimilate digital thought leaders from all across the world. We would then intersect them with our enterprise executives over one-and-a-half days of the summit. It was an explosive, interactive, no-holds-barred event. The idea was to stir up debate within the leadership on the disruptive potential of the digital era and its impact on their business models.

The engagement with start-ups is highly symbiotic. Start-ups need enterprise use cases to try out and improve their innovations. Enterprises need the freshness of the start-up mindset and their solutions to open up the enterprise mindset to the art of the possible. Both can benefit from each other. So, go ahead and forge a bridge between the two worlds. You will see a cost efficient and effective relationship emerge between them if the connectivity is orchestrated properly.

Also, build capability for in-house experimentation. You can use a community approach for building this capability. Instead of dedicating resources to the entire innovation pipeline, the initial few stages can be undertaken by an internal community of passionate contributors wanting to learn new stuff. If the innovation survives through to the later stages of the pipeline, you can then augment the community with full time resources. Very similar to an open-source community but incubated, nurtured and deployed internally.

Hackathons, remote innovation outposts, university relationships, incubators, innovation labs, all represent nodes of a vibrant innovation ecosystem and capability. It need not cost you a whole lot of money to build, if done right, but it is a key underpinning capability on which to nurture your transformation. What this capability yields is perceptual acuity, i.e., acumen over your perceptions, the ability to see around corners through experimentation, to build foresight and then scale those experiments which yield initial results. This acumen is a great capability and asset to have through your transformation journey.

Cyber security

The entire digital transformation journey can come to a grinding halt with one debilitating cyber security incident. This is especially true in the case of existing large enterprises which have built a brand and reputation over several years of toil. You have to invest in the yang of cyber security along with the yin of digital. Again, this is a critical internal capability and there is no option. As soon as you open digital channels for your customers to experience, you also increase the vulnerability to attack. Hence you need to put in mitigating controls to reduce the risk. Let us be clear. You can never eliminate completely the cyber security risks. The hacker is no longer the quintessential kid in the garage hacking away to glory. There are now fairly sophisticated actors involved in cyber-crime and espionage. In addition, this is another field of technology going through rapid transformation. Every day there is a new threat and a new invention to counter it.

Your cyber security capability should ideally follow a layered approach. Defence in depth. All three phases of attack – pre-compromise, compromise and post-compromise – should be well within scope and relevant tech deployed to mitigate the risks at each phase. While the details of the cyber security tech stack are not within the scope of my endeavour, suffice to say that this is a fairly sophisticated capability which should include both internal resources, ably augmented by external experts. Your ideal chief information security officer (CISO) is someone who has deep exper-tise in this area, but also someone who can simplify and explain in business terms the risks and what is being done to mitigate them.

Change management

We have all heard the cliché 'change is the only constant'. But it is one of those rare clichés which is so very true. We live in a constantly changing world. Not many things are deterministic now. As enterprises, as individuals and leaders we have to develop the capability to manage change effectively. There is no way around this. There is no point burying your head in the sand and assuming that the current wave of change will pass you by. The fact remains, that even if it does, there is a bigger wave of change succeeding it, at a faster pace than before.

I have encapsulated my experience in managing change into the following change mantras, which if adopted will help hone the ability to deal with this constant barrage of change.

The burning platform

Most change initiatives need a burning platform to ignite the change and break the inertia. In my experience, if such a platform exists, great, use it. If it does not exist, create it. Having said that, the fact is that in current times, we are bombarded with burning platforms every day. It is about honing the ability to sense these and then use them to kick off the change process.

Strategy > process > structure > people

In my experience, I have seen leaders use change management as a euphemism to conduct organizational change or sometimes just to fire people. This is fundamentally incorrect. Any change process should first start with definition of the strategy, proceed to defining the new processes in alignment with the strategy, then collate processes and capabilities into organization structure and only then review if the people capability matches with the needs of the new organization structure. It should always work left to right, from strategy to people and not the other way round.

A strong internal coalition

Changes take time to come to affect. During the duration, there will be innumerable occasions where the doubters will try and derail the change process. It is critical at this time to have the support of a strong internal coalition. I was once tasked to institute an enterprise scale governance process which required over 20 senior executives to work together and take certain decisions. As part of the design process, we carefully worked on creating a strong internal coalition of a few of the executives and ensured their complete buy-in. I ran this process for over six years. I cannot recall how many times, when we were being challenged on the fundamentals, these 'good apples' as we had designated them among us, would stand up and quell any dissent. If it wasn't for the support of this internal coalition, there was no way this tricky change process would have survived and then run for six long years.

Pace over perfection

When it comes to transformative change, pace is definitely your friend. It is better to get the first results out, celebrate and make the change visible, as opposed to waiting for perfection and taking a long time to first result.

Leader led

Change is one of those disciplines which visibly needs for the leader to get involved. While in general I am a firm believer of non-hierarchical network organizations, in the case of change, the effort must be led from the top. The leadership team has to be the first one to adopt the change and ensure this adoption is highly visible in the organization. They should also be seen to be strong advocates of the change and involved with most communications about the change.

Communicate

This capability gets overlooked very often, but is critical to the success of change. We need to ensure a clear communications plan is crafted and then regimentally followed throughout the change process. In change programmes I have led or participated, we blocked two half-days for communications. One was blocked for the larger staff base where we would organize a weekly all-staff townhall to update them on the change and get any feedback. In addition, another half-day was to evangelize the change with key stakeholder groups within the enterprise. The more the communications and enterprise-wide engagement, the better the success of your change initiative.

Do. Feel. Think

The mantra of bias to action has seeped into every aspect of business and change – management is no exception. Earlier change practitioners would spend innumerable hours planning and the action would only start much later in the process. However, in my experience, we need to reverse this process. We need to break down the change into small tasks and get into action straight away with a small bit of the change, then feel the response to it, then think how best to scale to the next task. Do the change, feel its impact and then think about how to scale it further.

The words complicated and complex may mean the same when used colloquially; however, their difference is best explained through these two examples. If you are given the task to count the number of parts in an Airbus A380, that is a complicated task. However, you can still do it in a logical and algorithmic way and get to the answer. You can use the planning, the command-and-control paradigm to do this task. However, now if you are asked to unwind a nicely swirled up bowl of spaghetti, you will need to take hold of one end, slowly unwind, sense how the spaghetti is responding, then again unwind and go through this process till the entire bowl has been straightened up. Here, you will be deploying the sense-and-respond paradigm. All endeavours that involve human relationships are complex undertakings. Since change management is finally all about managing humans through the change process, it too falls under the complex paradigm and needs a sense-and-response method to get it across the line.

To consult or not

Our world is peppered with numerous models and frameworks on managing change, as well as with consultants and experts who can help with the process. I am sure those add value in some form or manner. However, in my experience, change is such an important core competency in today's business environment that the enterprise must develop the internal muscle to manage this on an ongoing basis. We cannot delegate the accountability of change to an external party. Yes, we can hire experts to help with the process; however, the accountability and management has to rest with internal enterprise leaders and teams.

Conclusion

These eight change mantras can help manage this complex, people-centric topic within large enterprises.

The Honeycomb approach is completed when the disruption of each cell, through the six Honeycomb nodes, is connected to the above six underpinning, enterprise-wide digital capabilities. If done properly and in consonance, my contention is that it will usher in a tipping point beyond which the organization will see an exponential impact on its current business as well as acquire an inherent capability to continuously evolve into new business models at the right time.

Having understood the Honeycomb approach, in the next chapter, let us examine how the approach can be applied to some key domains and how it can ignite exponential possibilities for incumbent enterprises.

04

Accelerated possibilities

Business model explosion

The Cambrian explosion was a tipping point in our evolution.

This is exactly the pattern being followed by business models. There is a Cambrian explosion of business models happening today. Before the dawn of the digital era, the spectrum of business models was relatively limited. The models were constrained by scarcity of resources and companies vied for economics of scale. Pipeline business models were predominant, where you converted scare resources into final products, which were distributed through brick-and-mortar channels. Then a tipping point arrived, and a tectonic shift happened. There has been a Cambrian explosion of business models in the last decade or so.

The likes of Disney shifted from selling family entertainment to selling experiences. The Disney magic brand and associated platforms helped the creation of an experience ecosystem around the Disney brand. User-generated content disrupted content creation, and this gave birth to completely new enterprises such as YouTube and Vimeo. Large pipeline businesses embraced the dichotomous idea of 'mass customization'. Adidas let customers design and purchase their own shoes and apparel: miadidas. It enabled people to customize shoes with various elements – people could mix and match colours and even have their own name printed on them. The 'as a service' business model was born and even products such as razors were converted to 'shave a service' by digital natives like Dollar Shave Club.

The business model of retail is experiencing a complete digital apocalypse. The headlines below reflect this massive upheaval of an established industry happening right in front of our eyes.

- Sears files for bankruptcy after years of turmoil, *The Washington Post*, 15 October 2018.[1]
- 'JCPenney could be kicked off the New York Stock Exchange because its stock is worth too little', *CNN Business*, 9 August 9 2019.[2]
- 'Barneys is closing 15 of its 22 stores after filing for bankruptcy. Here's the full list', *Business Insider*, 6 August 2019.[3]
- 'GNC could close up to 900 stores and slash its mall location count in half as the retail apocalypse roars on', *Business Insider*, 23 July 2019.[4]

Conversely, e-commerce giants and digital natives are not only growing exponentially but also re-imagining brick-and-mortar experiences. The headlines below reflect this exponential growth.

- 'The stock market now has two $1 trillion companies: Amazon and Microsoft', *CNN Business*, 11 July 2019.[5]
- 'Shopify cracks the e-commerce code, and its billionaire CEO's fortune doubles in just six months', *Forbes*, 20 August 2019.[6]
- 'Alibaba ramps up offline efforts. Internet giant opens first physical store of its cross-border shopping platform', *China Daily*, 21 April 2018.[7]
- 'Why digitally native brands keep opening physical stores', *Bloomberg News*, 22 October 2018.[8]

New peer-to-peer business models emerged wherein individuals exchange products and services directly with each other with algorithms helping with the matching and exchange. Airbnb rose from nowhere to beat all incumbent hospitality brands hands down in terms of growth and valuations. New lingo like 'free-mium' entered the business vocabulary when brands such as LinkedIn grew exponentially by offering basic services free and charging for premium add-ons.

Although there has been an explosion of business models, the platform business model had the most profound impact in the digital era.

Brian Arthur's seminal 1996 article in the *Harvard Business Review* highlighted the tectonic shift from supply driven econo-mies of scale to demand driven increasing returns, driven by network effects.[9] That perspective and insightful postulation underpins the strategic shift in the digital era from pipeline to plat-form business models.

The inherent scarcity of physical resources results in constraints in supply as traditional companies scale, finally yielding the diminishing return curve. On the other hand, digital resources are infinitely abundant. Hence, they pose no such constraints, finally yielding increasing returns as network effects kick in and result in the winner taking most markets.

Both in market valuations and outcomes, platform business models are eating traditional pipeline models for lunch.

At the heart of platforms is a value creating interaction. This interaction needs to be orchestrated for network effects. The keyword here is orchestration. The core value within the interac-tion is created by the participants of the network and not the owner of the platform. This is a deep shift in role which incumbent enter-prises find difficult to deal with. The platform owner only provides the infrastructure, the factory floor and ensures quality of interac-tions. The participants are the ones who actually create value using this factory floor.

As described by author and expert Sangeet Paul Choudary,[10] the platform must provide three key capabilities: craft incentives, provide the factory floor, and play match maker for both sides of the marketplace. Efficiency of the financial incentive design is critical to ensuring a profitable scale out for platform companies. In today's clamour for growth, valuation and abundant capital, this efficiency is being neglected. Future proofing this business model demands a balance between growth and efficiency, which is surely going to be the predominant pattern for success in the future. Another indirect incentive is the inherent fear of missing out (FOMO) that takes root in the participants of both sides of the marketplace. Hence the owner needs to design the platform for this FOMO and virality. The whole art of growth hacking has its roots in the need to drive virality.

New generation technology is key to executing the platform business model. The factory floor for platform business models is the cloud. Data and advanced AI, and especially the recent advances in deep learning, underpin the matching capability for platform owners. Digital marketing along with social drives virality and growth hacking. Sensors enable sentience for platforms, contributing to more personalized incentives as well as real-time and relevant match making. Additionally, mobile is the channel for participation in the platform, to both produce and consume value.

If your pipeline has not been hit by a platform yet, it is only a matter of time. The tipping point for platforms has long been reached. Platforms are the new engines of the digital era and technology is its fuel. They work on exponential growth trajectories and result in 'winner takes most' market paradigms. Get your business on an exponential curve before it is too late.

But how is again the key question and the quandary. I strongly believe the Honeycomb framework provides a method to not only achieve exponential performance in exiting business models, but also for incumbent enterprises to launch new business models.

Do not get me wrong, this is going to be extremely difficult. New business model invention 'from within' is the closest to a mission impossible you will get. If entrepreneurship is tough, the tough get humbled when it comes to interpreneurship.

I evaluated two predominant patterns for incubating new business models within a large enterprise and both of them are fraught with impossibilities! You could incubate and then grow the new business model away from the mothership, with a brand-new digital team. Alternatively, you could bake it within the large enterprise in the same location. If you select the former, when you try to integrate the new business model you will be hit severely with the 'not invented here' syndrome. If you select the latter, the antibodies and immune system of the existing business model may kill any new model before its birth.

As I said earlier, the Honeycomb approach provides a way forward. The key to unlock this quandary are the capabilities you have nurtured as part of the Honeycomb method. From a technology perspective, you may not have custom developed a new tech platform fully, but the gateway API capability provides you enough horsepower to launch new digital products and business models. The Perceptual Acuity capability will help you conduct fast experiments on emergent business models and then decide which ones to scale further. The community of passion capability (see Chapter 3) as well as your investment in the academy will have built enough internal people capability and an open/curious mindset to invite and then scale new business models with open arms. The 'not invented here' syndrome will have been muted as a result of the visible celebration of the teams and their achievements. The data collected and the AI capability on top of it will help you launch and evaluate new business models with unprecedented levels of precision. Customer obsession will have seeped deep into your organization's soul and will underpin the launch of any new model. The tectonic shift in mindset towards openness and collaboration will enable new forms of thinking. For example, you may see unfair advantage and competitive moats in your customers, distribution, IP, brand, infrastructure, when coupled with strategic partnerships with nimble and digital native start-ups. This new perspective on your existing business coupled with an openness towards a partnering approach with outside disrupters may be one way to launch new business models.

In essence, the capabilities that you have matured as part of the Honeycomb approach provide the platform on which you can launch your new business model. If those capabilities have been well honed, it matters less whether you incubate within or outside. In fact, incubation of new business models and then scaling those that work becomes a standard process in your operating model. Transformation from within – a mission impossible – is now a more possible mission with the help of the Honeycomb approach.

Antifragile leadership

Culture is a derived variable. You cannot impact it directly. You have to act on a number of aspects of your enterprise and then a new culture starts dawning organically. Leadership is one such aspect. It sets the tone of the organizational culture.

Typically, in large enterprises it is the leadership which is most mired in legacy. This legacy is evident in the narratives spoken or unspoken. On the technology front, for example, the following are my top five leadership narratives which strangulate digital mindsets:

1 'Let us benchmark our IT investments with peers in the industry!'

2 'We are not a technology company!'

3 'IT, please fix the basics first.'

4 'All this tech jargon is not relevant to us!'

5 'Let us talk ROI and not Java!' (Sounds like a proper narrative, wait for my counter below.)

Let us take a closer look at each of these in turn.

Let us benchmark our IT investments with peers in the industry!

The fetish for benchmarks is the bane of a legacy enterprise's existence. It demotes everyone to the lowest common denominator. My closest legacy competitor, who will probably go out of business in the next two years, spends 2 per cent of annual revenue on IT – that's that then. This is the divine number that we need to evaluate ourselves against, or even better. The 'industry' benchmark hovers around 1.8 per cent, so that is our magical number. No one has any clue or cares about the recipe underpinning this magical industry benchmark. Research companies make money from these benchmarks and enterprises make legacy.

We are not a technology company!

Yes, I agree. Not every company is a technology company. I am not a fan of such statements from C-level enthusiasts as 'We are a technology company that happens to sell real estate', 'We are a technology company that happens to sell fashion', etc. Good for the press, not much help in changing culture.

There are no issues with acknowledging the soul of your business being aviation or real estate or anything else. However, executives typically use the tagline 'We are not a technology company' to avoid getting their hands and brains dirty with understanding the strategic and profound impact technology is having on their businesses. They choose to stay put at the shore with an earthquake imminent, as opposed to stepping outside their comfort zone to find new lands. It's a tagline so reflective of the inertia in leadership mindsets. No one is asking them to learn coding. However, understanding the impact of technology on their business models, on their very existence, is a core leadership responsibility in the digital era.

IT, please fix the basics first!

If IT only concentrates on fixing the tech legacy and debt in large enterprises, that work will continue long after someone has already disrupted your business model. This is such a typical linear mindset hang. One-dimensional thinking. Yes, of course basics need to be fixed and you cannot build the edifice of a digital business model on weak foundations; however, you need to do both, and at the same time. No one said disruption would be easy. There are frameworks available to manage the art of 'doing both'.

All this tech jargon is not relevant to us!

I do agree that there is too much jargon doing the rounds in the tech world and it confuses everyone. However, if you are a marketing professional, made chief marketing officer and then got promoted to CEO, you cannot say that 'ROI, margins, ROCE are all jargon, and I will not deal with them'. There are certain technology aspects which have a profound impact on your business and a basic understanding of those is your fiduciary duty as an executive team member. You are not expected to code or understand how cryptography works. However, you are expected to be vigilant about anything that impacts your business at the core. Whether you like it or not, certain technologies do fall in that category.

Let us talk ROI and not Java!

There is no doubt that IT folks need to talk business language. Many a consultant have made loads of money 'helping' IT and business bridge this gap. However, by using this argument excessively, business leaders overlook their own responsibility to make a genuine attempt to understand technology and its implications to business. It takes two to tango. If both business and IT teams made a genuine attempt to bridge this gap, it will get bridged.

Excessive focus on short-term inclined business metrics also leads to a mediocre culture in my view. Transformation is a long-term game. Yes, what gets measured gets done, so I am not advocating moving away from business metrics. It is the excessive focus on this narrative which acts as a barrier to authentic transformation. Miracles happen overnight, changes take time.

Leaders need to shed these narratives and put them in cold storage. They do not help the cultural transformation. Digital companies create new benchmarks and set the tone of the industry. They do not follow. You need not be a technology company but it critical for you to get close to the strategic impact of technology on your business. Do not use cliched narratives to avoid taking responsibility for digital in the digital era. Life in the digital era cannot be sequential. 'I will fix the basics first, take some rest and then start my transformation journey!' By the time you do all this sequentially, there may not exist an enterprise to transform. Do both. Commence both journeys together. You never know which jargon is going to disrupt your business. If you are in the forecasting markets business, Augur with its distributed roots may make your business model infeasible. If you are in any business, a new upstart leveraging OpenAI's GPT-3 may re-imagine your business and run it completely autonomously. If you are in the retail business, you are already facing extinction from your digital native brethren. Keep your friends close, and your enemies even closer. Get close to the tech jargon and ensure you are evaluating them for impact to your business model and existence. Get the technology experts to speak business knowledge but also make best efforts to learn tech. Don't learn Java, sure, but understand what impact the next algorithm written on it can have on your business.

Let us examine leadership from the lens of the Honeycomb nodes. Powered by short-term incentives and quarterly pressures, customer obsession typically takes a back seat in the C-suite. There is a tendency to glance over the customer related indicators on balance scorecards, in the wake of the heavy hitting and turbulence causing financial metrics. Customer experiences reside more within anecdotal stories as opposed to NPS scores. Leaders who spend time experiencing their customer's journeys and then recounting those experiences in team meetings are a rare breed. When done, this has a profound impact on the importance of customer obsession in the overall priorities of the enterprise.

I have been part of a few boardroom sessions where CEOs talk at great length, describing with a passion their customer journey experience and areas which need improvement. No metrics are involved – just a simple story of a customer's journey through the enterprise's processes and culture. The word spreads like wildfire right after the meeting is over. Not only do the immediate customer related issues get fixed immediately, but such a narrative also sets the tone that customer experience is important to us at the very top. Such stories and the ensuing action are important moments which slowly but surely spread the culture of customer obsession within legacy enterprise's large workforces.

I have always believed in a symbolic gesture to visibly bring the customer into every conversation. All meeting rooms should have one seat left free to symbolically represent the customer. Sometime during the meeting, the attendees should turn to this symbolic customer and then discuss/debate how what was discussed in the meeting adds value to the customer. Having a clear and visible line of sight to customer value contributes to enabling a customer obsessed culture.

The core of customer obsessed culture is of course about ensuring that the product or service offered has been designed and delivered based on customers' needs and wants, including latent ones, and to connect with customers emotionally. Just doing that is enough to get you off to the races. To win in the race, however, leaders need to become customer role models continuously and visibly. They do so by measuring, by experiencing customer journeys themselves and then using narratives and symbolic gestures to ensure this love for customers seeps into the soul of the organizational culture.

When it comes to process and data, three messages/themes characterize legacy leadership mindsets: (1) this is the way it is done out here – you do not know our industry; (2) war stories on how a leader used his industry intuition to save the day; and (3) report rich, insight poor. Industry knowledge can become a significant barrier to transforming business processes, if not applied in a nuanced and careful way. I personally believe that back-office processes are largely industry agnostic, certain mid-office processes benefit from industry knowledge, and front office or customer experience processes are best designed keeping the customer in mind, as opposed to the industry. As Accenture says, customer expectations are liquid.[11] Customers expect the same digital experience from a legacy bank or airline or real estate company as they expect from Uber and Airbnb. So, customer experience processes are best designed keeping these digital natives in mind.

Leaders really need to kill the narrative that 'it is the way it is done out here, you do not know the industry'. Business processes are the means for delivering customer promises. If these do not get transformed, neither will customer experiences, nor the enterprise. All processes need to be examined from the lens of the digital era. They need to be examined from the lens of autonomy (self-driving ops), as well as simplified exponentially. Domain knowledge should be removed as a constraint on reimagining the core, and instead serve as an enabler for the competitive edge.

Leaders across industries become famous for their intuitive judgement and how decisive they are in the absence of adequate data and/or conflicting signals. It is for this reason perhaps, C-level rarely transcend industries and only move from one company to another within the same industry, their intuition being cemented with every stint. This is also the reason that they do not see the tsunami of disruption coming! To be clear, I have nothing against leadership intuition. After all, our brain is the most complex and efficient computer, so why not utilize all its capabilities? The risk is in using intuition and past knowledge as the only guide to forge the path for the future. It is critical that leadership culture imbibes a sense of humility and gets away from this alpha male, 'I know it all' archetype. I would rather abide by the adage 'in intuition and God we trust, but first bring along some data'! It is not about ignoring intuition, but first getting a wide range of perspectives – from data, from insights, from AI, from outside in, from customers, from the edges – and then augmenting this panoramic perspective with human intuition to take a sound decision.

How many times have you heard leaders proudly proclaim, 'We started our digital transformation journey and within the first six months we have delivered 126 dashboards' or CTOs getting carried away with the business intelligence technology stacks from Oracle Express to Snowflakes? The fact is, however, that most legacy enterprises remain data rich and insight poor. We concentrate more on producing reports than on producing insights. There are just too many reports. The leaders need to radically simplify this whole domain and authentically espouse the principle of less is more. The key here is adoption followed by action. Firstly, my experience has been that 80 per cent of those dashboards are used 5 per cent of the time, and when they are used, no one does anything based on these reports. Leaders should adopt the 'so what' mantra when it comes to reporting and business intelligence. This will yield action from the KPIs and finally business value.

While mindset is a topic which goes well beyond leadership, the fact remains that leaders have a critical role in setting the culture and mindset of enterprises. My favourite digital mindset attributes for leaders are:

- If a leader lacks humility, he/she should run a hackathon or any crowdsourcing event. It is a truly humbling experience to learn how many diverse novel ideas, insights and business models the crowd can produce, *and* in your area of expertise! The first digital mindset attribute of a leader then is this willingness to learn and support a continuous outside-in ethos. Being open to new ideas, interested in trends and issues well beyond the focus of the company and industry.

• An adjacent attribute is perpetual curiosity and intrigue. In the digital era, the paranoid may survive, but the curious are the ones who will thrive. There should be a willingness to challenge the status quo and assumptions which form the edifice of incumbent business models.

• Velocity is speed, but with direction. A leader needs to set the direction based on a deep purpose and then have the mindset to speed everything up. Time is a precious commodity. Leaders should set the pace and speed up the dial of their enterprises on a continuous basis.

• A digital leader needs to set bold 'stretch' goals that require release of old ways of thinking to achieve them. They need to have a passion for getting things done. Dreams without deadlines are hallucinations and achieve nothing of value. A delivery-oriented mindset is critical for transformation to actually happen.

• And last but not least, a leader is no longer a sole crusader but an orchestrator of networks. A mindset which seeks out and builds a strong global network and then leverages it to get things done is another critical element of the digital mindset.

Leaders also need to visibly support and imbibe agile ways of working. As I explained earlier, we are not talking about the agile methodology for developing software. We do not want our leaders to become scrum masters, but we do need the leaders to understand and appreciate the revolution an agile mindset brings to the corporate culture. The ability to break down work into smaller components and then direct smaller, autonomous teams to deliver each component can be applied to several disciplines of an enterprise. Leaders need to shun this mindset which relegates agile to IT and take inspiration from enterprises such as ING and their agile transformation journeys. Instead of having long-winded executive meetings, where politics and one-upmanship dictate the proceedings, leaders should imbibe practices such as daily stand-ups where everyone is focused on the outcome and scarcity of time focuses the updates to what is truly essential. Setting a very clear purpose, the hallmark of all agile teams, and then rallying the troops around that purpose. Frequent planning sessions, which take into consideration the fast-changing context of the digital era.

For years, I have tried to keep teams connected through an interactive form of communications, which we termed as 'vernissages'. This was not a term I invented, but something I learned from a boutique management consultancy based in Germany. The pattern is similar to a marketplace after a hackathon, where teams set up their stands and then update everyone on their deliverables. Communications is such an important component of a leader's responsibility and critical to the transformation journey. Digital leaders need to adopt innovative ways to ensure a two-way dialogue with the larger workforce. They need to take ownership and drive the communications themselves and not see it as a burden on their already heavy shoulders.

Leaders need to understand and then lead the journey to cloud architectures and ways of working. The cloud gives them the ability to orchestrate distributed global teams using the cloud – the ability to scale up and scale down their needs and hence costs, based on cloud's pay-as-you-go commercial model. Given the variability that exists in our business environment today, the elasticity the cloud provides to business operations is a very useful capability to have. The ability to innovate at low cost and fail fast plus fail forward, enabled by the cloud architecture, are all paradigms the leader needs to appreciate and get close to. This is not only for your IT person to sort out. This is for you to understand, gauge its risk and its strategic opportunity, and then drive within your enterprise, as true leaders do.

Antifragile is not only about embracing change or bouncing back after a change hits you. Antifragile is about developing a leadership muscle which allows you to improve with every change event. I firmly believe that leaders who go through these Honeycomb nodes and hone their capabilities as described above will develop their antifragile muscle. And once leaders develop this muscle, eventually so does the organization. The visible role model and their attributes will rub off on all other staff and slowly but surely the culture will become much more digital. I don't think we can impact culture directly. However, developing role model leaders and then visibly celebrating outcomes will create a movement within your organization. Each win will feed that movement. Wins and achievements have a way to go viral. Before long, most will be singing from the same cultural hymn sheet, and those who just can't will move on to write another song or join another orchestra.

Autonomous ops

There is no doubt in my mind that the world of enterprise operations in the future will be autonomous. A self-driving, invisible ops for autonomous enterprises. This future is here already, it is just not evenly distributed. The human-free Amazon or Alibaba warehouse is the harbinger of what is coming to a mid-office and back-office near you. After all, robots are only the extrovert avatars of the introvert machine learning and AI algorithms. If a warehouse can run fully autonomously why cannot the same level of autonomy apply to an 'order to cash' or 'procure to pay' process? Understandably, the first applications of AI have been in the visible customer experience space. However, you cannot have a digital veneer and an analogous back office. This is not 'being' digital. This is not 'authentic' transformation. The back office must be (a) synchronized in real time with the promises made to customers through the digital channels, and (b) run autonomously for exponentially efficient operational performance.

Let's examine what needs to be done in the processes, technology and people nodes of the Honeycomb approach in order to achieve the invisible operations vision for enterprises.

The operational processes need to be reimagined. However, this time around do not invite the traditional consultants in to do the classical business process re-engineering. First and foremost, look at the processes from the lens of AI and technology. Technology/ AI first, then people and then the process itself. The AI and technology first approach will allow you to discover the art of the possible with respect to process design itself and consequently, achieve exponential simplification and automation.

One can envisage a world today where for high volume, low value items, a swarm of coordinated bots create automatic requisitions, place them in a blockchain based open marketplace, negotiate with multiple supplier agent bots, place orders, receive goods and finally pay, all with limited to no human interference. An autonomous procure to pay ecosystem. Your bot swarms can be set an overall business objective – say, optimize costs as well as time to procure – and then they can use reinforcement learning to create the most simplified and efficient pathway to achieving the objectives set. No need for humans to sit down with pen and pencil and design a simplified process. Let the bot swarms do that for you, using real data and context. Augment them with your ingenuity and innovation, but let the AI and tech go first.

When I was in the aviation world, our flight planning application used to produce certain flight plans autonomously. There was no human interaction. These were for the routine routes that met certain operational criteria which had already been fed into the system. However, when it comes to our back-office processes, we refuse to do anything autonomously. Even when an invoice has been auto matched perfectly, as per all company policies including the three-way or four-way match, we still want someone to review it and approve! With significant advancement in computer vision as well as adoption of back-office cloud native applications which allow your supplier network to upload invoices using a simple browser, we should be able to get near 100 per cent autonomous operation of this activity. Manual reconciliation processes should be eliminated. Bots are much better in reconciling than humans and they can work 24/7 non-stop. The tech exists – it is the mindset and the drive that is sometimes missing in legacy enterprises.

Similarly, the talent acquisition process, from sourcing to onboarding new staff, is quite arduous in legacy enterprises. Humans also suffer from a host of cognitive biases. Some of them definitely interfere with an objective evaluation of who is best for the role. AI enabled bots can augment both the quality and speed of the 'source to onboard' process. They can raise anticipatory recruitment requests based on data such as turnover rate, actual resignations, etc. and create the demand profile based on job descriptions. They can then go on an invisible talent hunt, scrounging internal and external data sets such as LinkedIn to look for matching candidates. The initial screening can also be delegated to the AI bots, who can screen, rank and shortlist candidates. Humans can come in at this point and conduct the final selection. From thereon, the offer management and onboarding process formalities can be managed by the bots. If done properly, a consonance of bots and humans can exponentially impact this time consuming but vital back-office process.

There is that issue of bias in AI though. This needs to be considered very carefully and the data set used for training your AI needs to cover all personas and demographics, with a clear objective to remove any bias. The whole field of explainable AI is also important so that we can understand what happens within the AI black box and include adequate controls so that bias is mitigated from the outcomes.

Entrenched, legacy technology will definitely be a barrier to your invisible ops endeavour. In the airline world, you have the legacy passenger services systems (PSS), the revenue optimization commercial applications, the flight operations suite of typically third-party applications, the standard ERPs (enterprise resource planning) for your support process automations. In the real estate world, you have the property management systems running alongside ERPs to automate the core operations. In hospitality again you have the legacy PMSs running alongside a slew of niche solutions. In the manufacturing world, you typically have the ERPs at the core of ops. What is common amongst all these applications across all these industries? They were all designed and delivered well before the dawn of the AI era. Approaches like robotic process automation have evolved; however, they emulate what humans do and do not reimagine operational processes from the lens of AI and technology. These legacy applications are deeply entrenched in the business and operating models of most industries, and even more so in the legacy mindsets, who have operated and internalized these systems through the industrial era. The tech landscape in operations is a significant barrier to your autonomous vision, and you will have to deal with it.

As discussed earlier, two approaches are possible for transforming these operational applications. You can choose the right one based on your individual business context and appetite. Find the money, the stakeholder alignment and the right strategic partner ecosystem to rebuild the core from the start, with an AI first approach. This will get you the biggest bang for your buck when it comes to making exponential, systemic, sustainable change. And do not try to do this fully on your own. The airline industry graveyards are brimming with failed attempts to rewrite the core reservations platform! Do it with likeminded partners, including perhaps a large investor, who has the same ethos and strategic vision as you for true transformation. In the hospitality industry, for example, there are proper cloud native platforms now available for front-office, mid-office and back-office processes. A number of these platforms also embed AI deeply into them. In such cases, I suggest pushing and influencing and building the business cases to change the core platforms to their modern versions.

The other approach is of course to 'hollow the existing core' – leave it to do the bare minimum transaction work, build a world of APIs above this hollowed core and then write your AI algorithms in an AI layer about the APIs. As long as the APIs allow a two-way, real-time interaction between the AI layer and the hollow core, you should be good in the interim. Eventually, you will have to replace the core, but this approach will allow you to show business value through rapid accomplishments, which will in turn help you finally get the funding to replace the core. I was involved with slowly stripping an Airline's passenger reservation system of its functionality, including a fairly large carve out of its search and shopping capability into a modern, cloud native application. We then left the mainframe to only do the inventory bit, which, to be honest, it was quite good at handling.

Not to be disingenuous to them, but in my experience the people mindset in operations will be the most difficult challenge in your transformation journey. The fossilization of legacy culture and mindset has occurred over years of evolution. The tools and technology available have reinforced that mindset further. People are entrenched in their ways of working and not willing to change. That is how flights are dispatched every hour, crew rosters built every month, rates loaded into hospitality PMSs, three-way invoice matching done, requisitions raised and delivered, production planning done, property service requests planned and delivered. That is the way this world has worked for centuries and this is the way it gets done here. You need to get in there and rip this comfort zone apart. The earlier re-imagination of processes will definitely result in requiring fewer humans to run operations. Use that as an impetus to identify and select your most disruption-ready mindsets using the phoenix process. Additionally, infuse some young and fresh external talent into the mix, then use the capability of the digital academy to ignite their disruption passions and strengthen their transformation muscles. This three-step architecture of selection, infusion and academy will help create a strong and fit team to lead your invisible ops journey.

The bottom line is that AI has reached its tipping point for deployment in the enterprise, and it can make a large part of your back office autonomous. In the past, your mid- and back-office applications would be a constraint to achieving autonomy; however, now a number of industries have seen the emergence of cloud native applications which either embed AI in them or can work easily with an AI layer built by the enterprise. People and mindset is a huge issue, especially in operations, but you can fix that at pace using the phoenix process.

The time is ripe, the tech is ready to go, so get on with it.

Algorithmic marketing and selling

The marketing, sales, customer engagement, customer care, customer service and other such functions in new age enterprises need to be personalized *to* the customer. Also, they need to be personalized *with* the customer, so that there is a two-way dialogue and not just a one-way monologue which determines how the personalization should work. Exotic marketing personas determined by the enterprise which typecast the customer into a box are passé and not going to work in the future. You need to connect with the customer and their context in real time, in an always-on mode.

How do you connect with every individual customer, always, based on their live context, when you could be taking about millions of customers of a large enterprise? This is no mean feat.

It cannot be achieved by following the traditional approaches to these customer-facing enterprise functions. You stand a better chance if you use the holistic approach of the Honeycomb and transform all the six nodes through a concerted transformation push.

The first step in this journey requires assimilation of customer data. The privacy debate, along with associated regulatory barriers, will rise to confront you as soon as you start on this pathway. Tackle this topic head on. Turn customer privacy into a core value and mission of your initiative and a passion for your enterprise. After all, you are collecting data with the genuine purpose of servicing your customers and delighting them in their experiences with you. Let your authenticity be known to your customers. Make your intent radically transparent to them. Seek their consent boldly with this authentic mindset. Extract out consent statements from the fine print and bring them up-front, close and personal.

Start collecting data into the standard data lake architecture. Collect everything you can. Remember that data has an options value and in this customer domain, definitely so. To get to an ultra level of personalization, you need all the data you can lay your hands on. Also dial in the clock to real-time processing. Attention spans have been shrinking for humanity and loyalty has become ephemeral. Customers look out for and value delightful moments and not long-drawn-out engagements. It is important to have the real-time data and insight to be able to spring those delightful surprises on your customers. Also, set up your data architecture to provide for infinite horizontal (attributes) and vertical (number of customers) scale. Data algorithms will eventually work on filling up both these dimensions in your data lake. Create a de-coupled architecture for the AI layer which allows you to buy and deploy specialist data enhancing algorithms from specialist partners as well as build your own algorithms.

The other big shift in this domain is that all these functions are becoming fully digitized. This trend is driven largely by the consumers. They prefer the ease of engaging through digital channels – for service, or commerce or indeed for consuming marketing content relating to your enterprise. You must follow suit or risk losing them to competition. This large-scale digital migration provides a unique opportunity to radically re-imagine customer facing processes and organizational structures.

Let's look at organizational structures for a moment. Typically, a large enterprise has at-least three direct customer facing functions if not more – marketing, sales and customer service. Any chance of providing delightful moments of experience are lost in the crevices of these silos. This broken organizational architecture manifests itself starkly in the e-commerce sites of the legacy enterprise. The internal fights for space and glory as well as the internal power structure, so visible in either the pre-eminence of brand content or functionality on the e-commerce channel. There is a perpetual debate between the marketing and e-commerce heads on who owns the channel and what goes into it.

These silos should be broken down into one team with one mission – the customer. Also reduce the number of C-level executives across all these customer facing roles. Over the years, too many C's have appeared in the fabric of executive teams: Chief Commercial, Chief Marketing, Chief Customer, Chief Data, Chief Growth. Collapse all of these into one or two roles, with end-to-end responsibility for the customer.

Deeply intertwine the marketing processes into sales and vice versa. Let the data collected earlier and the customer insights from it permeate into all activities across a unified customer facing process. Let there be one agile squad at the operational level which markets, sells and services the customer. Rotate team members into respective roles within each squad so that they fully appreciate the need for an integrated approach to managing customers as well as leads/prospects. You may ask aren't these highly specialist roles, how can these be done within one agile squad? Look at new age marketing. You will hear specialist terms such as SEO, social marketing, influencer marketing, creative content creation, campaign management, PPC, etc. How can someone in a team rotate into these specialist roles? Well, there is an interesting characteristic of the digital era. College has become expensive and education has become free! Put a team together and include in this team digital mindsets with a passion for the customer. They will together sort all these specialisms out. You can learn digital marketing online without paying a single dime, as long as the learning intent exists.

After the radical simplification of the organizational structure and people architecture, the processes too need a complete overhaul. There are two dimensions on which the business processes in this domain need to be transformed. Firstly, the deep digitization of all processes through automation followed by an AI driven autonomous boost. Be it content management, lead generation and nurturing, campaign management, contact centre operations, customer service operations, selling, there is absolutely no reason why core technology platforms along with AI algorithms cannot automate these processes. It is just a matter of mindset. The technology already exists. If the will exists, you can aim for and deliver radical automation and nearly human-free operation for each of these sales, marketing and customer service business processes.

The second dimension is perhaps even more important. As all the mundane tasks and more run autonomously, concentrate the human effort on creating an emotional connect with your customers. That should be the sharp focus of all the humans working on customer-facing processes: to orchestrate the creation of content which connects the customers emotionally to the brand; to create campaigns which appeal to individual needs and sensitivities; to reach out to leads and work with them through an emotionally connected journey as they go deeper into the sales cycle and convert to paying customers; and finally, to fans or advocates. Ensure that every service contact with the customer expresses an ethos of love, empathy and genuine care for the customer.

Both these strategic shifts in the customer-facing business processes, i.e., extreme and radical automation on one hand and human emotional connects on the other, lend themselves to unprecedented levels of personalization to the specific needs of the customers. Intent mining algorithms can further help with giving valuable insights into the context of your customer, to further personalize the interaction based on the specifics of that context.

So that is what you have got to do. Use advanced technology and real-time data to radically automate your customer facing business processes, annihilate the complexity by radically simplifying the organizational architecture, build agile squads which squeeze out all crevices of the erstwhile functional silos, and fine-tune the people competence to only focus on building a deeper, meaningful and personal emotional connect with every customer. Not for the faint hearted, but definitely feasible in the digital era we live in. If done right, you will not only have transformed your relationship with your customers but also created an unsurmountable competitive moat.

The Covid catalyst

In the year since I have been penning down this book, humanity has faced one of its biggest challenges – Covid-19, the pandemic. In a single stroke, the virus has impacted individuals, societies, economies, businesses, supply chains, globally and at an immense pace. The entire world has been brought to a standstill. The virus has not spared anyone. The impact of the virus has been far reaching.

On the digital front though, Covid has definitely acted as a strong catalyst and an accelerator of digital transformation. As country after country announced stringent lockdowns, digital distribution models and e-commerce surged. Traditional enterprises which operated only brick and mortar models had to rush to launch digital capabilities. Consequently, there has been an exponential surge in the adoption of e-commerce during the Covid period. Online demand surged across the world for all sorts of categories from building supplies, hobby/office supplies, personal care products, clothing, shoes, jewellery and across all services from teaching, coaching and interior design to home grooming. Those who are not able to cope and have not built the organizational capability to adapt fast are folding up. Those who are agile and nimble and have invested in digital capabilities are able to adjust to the new reality, launch new business and/or distribution channels and survive. The Honeycomb approach recommends engaging with customers through digital channels. It urges enterprises to build fully-fledged digital products and not just websites and apps. Those enterprises which had the foresight to build these capabilities are definitely faring better during the pandemic than those which ignored the writing on the wall and submerged their heads in the sand.

Covid-19 resulted in a deep decline in revenues. As an airline executive remarked to me, zero is also a single digital number when it comes to load factors! With revenue tending to zero, there is no way that enterprises could sustain without yanking significant costs out of their operations. In addition, the sudden need for contactless operations added another layer of complexity to an already dire undertaking. The only way to exponentially reduce cost, while not exponentially reducing customer service, is to first automate your operations and then make it autonomous. The marginal cost of deploying an additional bot to do work is near zero.

The Honeycomb approach recommends a strong focus on making your operations invisible, through deployment of automation and AI. Those that had focused on making their back-office digital are definitely more able respond to the sudden vaporization of the top line. To give you a simple, but practical example: almost all large enterprises have an authority's manual in which approval authority rests with a few senior executives. Given that courts still demand wet ink on most contractual documentation, large enterprises have typically not digitized simple approval workflows and various documents still need wet signatures. Now imagine during the peak of Covid-19 as executives stayed at home, someone had to travel around to their homes, carrying the documents that needed their physical signatures. The execs had to come out of their homes, wearing masks, and then sign these documents, carefully sanitizing themselves before and after the signing was done. This had to be repeated for each signature for required, for every document!

The alternative was for enterprises to be proactive on digital transformation, ensure background work was done with all stakeholders, including regulatory authorities, so that digital signatures were accepted, and the relevant capability deployed. These are the simple but effective things that make a difference. Not just having a digital veneer but ensuring your back offices are sufficiently digitized, as well as in sync with the front office, to be able to deliver the promise to your internal and external customers. Covid definitely accelerated the adoption of digital in back office and mid office operations.

The Honeycomb approach recommends a quantum shift in the ways of working, driven by technology. As mentioned earlier, one component of tech-related disruption recommended by the Honeycomb approach is to shift business processes to the Cloud. Imagine those who had not taken this leap before Covid. Most enterprises had to shift to mass remote working, over a weekend, as lockdowns came into effect. For decades, nothing happens and then in a week a decade happened. If your tech landscape, including workplace services, was not running on the cloud, you would have been in a royal pickle! For those that had deployed workplace and collaboration tools on the Cloud, and embraced distributed and federated architectures, it was amazing how the entire workforce seamlessly shifted to remote working over a few working days. Stories will be told for years after Covid-19 is done and dusted about how staff went remote and perhaps a large number of them never came back to the office – all enabled by proper and proactive deployment of distributed architectures across the technology landscape.

Covid has also accelerated new and disruptive digital, business models. In healthcare, the telehealth business model expanded exponentially across the globe. The lockdowns limited access to in-person healthcare services, and this resulted in a surge in tele-medicine adoption by patients. Additionally, a host of start-ups started novel attempts to solve the 'test, cure and prevent' trio challenge for the coronavirus. The amount of innovation in this space has been exponential through the Covid period and will have a long-lasting collateral benefit for healthcare in the longer term.

The banking world was already under attack from nimble Fintech start-ups. Pre-Covid, consumers were moving away from bank branches and during Covid people did not want to even go near an ATM. What started as a movement in the UK with open banking and London's Fintech hubs such as Canary Warf, have accelerated to South East Asia as well as the rest of the world with the rapid launch and adoption of digital banking services. Two types of players have been born: those that have a core banking license and then build digital banking services on top of the license – the challenger bank archetype; and those who are in the consumer lifestyle business and have leveraged their existing consumer base to launch banking services in partnership with a bank who already has a license – the neo bank archetype. Launch and adoption of both archetypes have accelerated across the globe due to Covid.

The retail apocalypse continues and speeds up with Covid. As footfall dried up in most brick-and-mortar shops, retailers had to respond with new distribution models, with a rapid-fire launch of e-commerce being the top response. If you had not built this digital capability in retail, you are probably out of business by now. In addition, adoption of new models such as 'click and collect' was accelerated through the pandemic. The Cloud kitchen business model has accelerated in the food and beverage industry, with delivery-only services. ClassPass, a subscription service for virtual fitness, grew its studio base exponentially during Covid. CNN acknowledged this shift in its headline coverage: 'The $94 billion fitness industry is reinventing itself as Covid-19 spreads'![12] A new dating app called 'Quarantine Together' was launched during these bizarre times.

A number of digital business models were also negatively impacted. There was an adverse impact on a number of sharing economy related business models. For instance, not many people wanted to go into a shared accommodation provided by the likes of Airbnb or indeed venture into common spaces of co-living and co-working provided by start-ups. I remember from a start-up pitch in Silicon Valley, where the founders had built a business out of sharing and renting designer dresses. I am sure such business models would have found it difficult to sustain funding during Covid. The reverberations of the pandemic were felt across the globe, across all industries spanning all business models.

The Honeycomb approach strongly recommends that large enterprises remain paranoid and continue to experiment with new business models. This helps develop the organizational muscle to move to a new business model, crisis or no crisis. Those who had developed the organizational capability and mindset to question the assumptions of their incumbent business models and pivot to new ones fared much better during Covid than those who were comfortable with the status quo.

As employees went 100 per cent remote, the need for deeper engagement with them became an imperative, right after resolving the technical challenge of getting them to work remotely was sorted. The feeling of community and camaraderie was even more important during this period. Executives around the globe increased both the cadence and intensity of connecting with their staff. The fact that everyone could assemble together, at the click of a button, from anywhere in the world helped a lot in keeping everyone engaged and motivated. Some forward-looking enterprises also built communities on topics like health and wellness, or ran entertainment sessions organized by staff for the staff, using internal resources.

The customer pillar of the Honeycomb approach is not just about creating great experiences for customers, but also about ensuring the employee's digital experience is modern and world class. Those who had invested in such employee platforms and ensured adoption across their employee base were able to provide innovative services to their employees, such as being able to order food and beverages through the platform at a discount and get them delivered to the home of staff in the case of a hospitality enterprise. Or if you are in the grocery business, being able to do same-day delivery of grocery items using the platform, at honest prices. Loyalty is not just about collecting points. It is about a deep, lasting emotional connection with the brand and its promise. Employee loyalty is no different. Those enterprises which had invested in cloud-based, remote-working workplace infrastructure, built new age digital platforms for employees and who leveraged these to build a strong emotional connection with their employees will definitely see an upsurge in loyalty, retention and discretionary effort going forwards.

I am part of a global community called the Exponential Organization (ExO). In normal times, we help enterprises think exponentially and seek disruptive solutions through a methodology called exponential sprints. During the early days of Covid, this passionate community of exponential thinkers organically got together to help solve some important aspects of the pandemic issue. It was brilliant, as community members across the world contributed significant amounts of their time and ran the exponential sprint method virtually to solve for the pandemic. The Honeycomb approach recommends communities of passion as a key underpinning capability for transformation. During Covid, the need and benefits of building employee communities though deeper engagement, or engaging larger human communities to solve big problems, became crystal clear.

AI and data were deployed across the globe to manage the core pandemic related processes and activities ranging from traceability, detection, therapeutic and then preventative. In each of these activities, AI augmented human endeavour to accelerate solutions for Covid. Besides being extremely useful in fighting the pandemic, AI came in very handy for those enterprises who had developed the AI capability and mindset. As brick-and-mortar retailers closed down, revenue dried up and cash piles depleted, retail executives needed real-time, accurate data for survival. Those who had nurtured and curated data as critical business assets were able to tune up the cadence to real time and provide both data and foresight to the executives. Supply chains globally got clogged and tied up working capital. AI was used to predict failure points in the supply chain, gain actionable insights and help mitigate the dire situation. Warehouse demand and hence pricing went up significantly, as almost everyone moved to e-commerce. Those with robotic pallet handling systems in the warehouses, underpinned by AI, were able to reduce both the time and cost of shipment processing. AI assisted route management ensured a much higher on-time delivery percentage as compared to those using traditional route optimization methods. As companies reduced their workforce significantly, it became even more important to perform business processes such as sales with enhanced precision. AI enabled lead nurturing or customer propensity models helped sales do much more with much less. Cash flow forecasting, dynamic resource allocation, upsell/cross sell opportunities, footfall analysis and numerous such enterprise use cases moved from theory to practice, again only for those who had followed some of the pathways recommended by the Honeycomb approach and developed the recommended underpinning capabilities for operating in the digital era.

Digital mindsets

Digital transformation is finally about mindset shift. A digital mindset manifests itself in adoption of new technologies, new ways of working and new business ideas. I believe that Covid has had the most profound impact on the adoption curve. As you are all aware, the change/adoption bell curve is quite well proven across all sorts of change efforts. A few innovators go first and adopt anything you throw at them. They are first off the blocks, highly curious and wanting to test out new stuff first. Then comes the rigid middle – a large chunk of stakeholders who watch and wait. If they see the winds shifting to the left, they join the innovators, else they resist the change effort and throttle it. Then, towards the end of the curve, are the cynics. They have a clear 'not invented here' syndrome and match it equally with the 'not happening here' paradigm. If they ever change, it is by force – someone literally dragging them towards the left.

Covid did not give anyone the chance nor the time to follow this well-established bell curve. For some companies, 100 per cent of the workforce had to move remote and use technology that enabled remote access to corporate services within a few days. There was no other way but to go digital. I believe this sudden and fast change has fundamentally shifted the adoption curve to the left. The rigidity of the middle has been shaken at the roots. As we come out of the pandemic, we need to (a) recognize this shift in the adoption/change management curve, and (b) further cement this opening especially amongst the rigid middle. If done properly, this will enable the new mindset to sustain and propagate, which will be the biggest benefit for any future transformation endeavour.

Covid barged into the edifices of command-and-control corporate architectures. These architectures and structures are predicated on static, low variability environments where you can neatly plan and structure your leadership responses. Within minutes, any short- and medium-term plans were no longer valid. Executives had to grapple with the full force of the VUCA world, which the digital era has for long ushered. They were forced to shift to a more agile, nimble, adaptive, 'sense and respond' mindset. And that is exactly the antifragile mindset that the Honeycomb approach recommends for leadership in the digital era. Covid gave all leadership teams across all industries and geographies live practice on working the digital mindset. We need to ensure this mindset sticks and is not ephemeral.

Acceleration is the bottom line. There is no simpler way to say it. Covid accelerated digital transformation across the globe. Those who have been proactive in building the capabilities identified in the Honeycomb approach are faring much better than those who did not.

Endnotes

1 Siegel, R (2018) 'Sears files for bankruptcy after years of turmoil', *The Washington Post*, 15 October. www.washingtonpost.com/business/2018/10/15/sears-nears-bankruptcy-after-years-turmoil/ (archived at https://perma.cc/PFM5-C464)

2 Isidore, C (2019) 'JCPenney could be kicked off the New York Stock Exchange because its stock is worth too little', *CNN Business*, 9 August. edition.cnn.com/2019/08/09/business/jcpenney-delisting/index.html (archived at https://perma.cc/2URM-3SWB)

3 Biron, B. (2019) 'Barneys is closing 15 of its 22 stores after filing for bankruptcy. Here's the full list', *Business Insider*, 6 August. www.businessinsider.in/barneys-is-closing-15-of-its-22-stores-after-filing-for-bankruptcy-heres-the-full-list-/articleshow/70558416.cms (archived at https://perma.cc/6C4Q-WQWK)

4   Taylor, K. (2019) 'GNC could close up to 900 stores and slash its mall location count in half as the retail apocalypse roars on', *Business Insider*, 23 July. www.businessinsider.in/gnc-could-close-up-to-900-stores-and-slash-its-mall-location-count-in-half-as-the-retail-apocalypse-roars-on/articleshow/70337652.cms (archived at https://perma.cc/6FQK-SY3B)

5   La Monica, P.R. (2019) 'The stock market now has two $1 trillion companies: Amazon and Microsoft', *CNN Business*, 11 July. edition.cnn.com/2019/07/11/investing/amazon-microsoft-trillion-dollar-market-value/index.html (archived at https://perma.cc/YMW8-GPUE)

6   Au-Yeung, A. (2019) 'Shopify cracks the e-commerce code, and its billionaire CEO's fortune doubles in just six months', *Forbes*, 20 August. www.forbes.com/sites/angelauyeung/2019/08/20/shopify-cracks-the-e-commerce-code-and-its-billionaire-ceos-fortune-doubles-in-just-six-months/?sh=309b15e77f57 (archived at https://perma.cc/9WG4-XHNJ)

7   He Wei, (2018) 'Alibaba ramps up offline efforts', China Daily, 2 April. www.chinadaily.com.cn/a/201804/21/WS5adaad92a3105cdcf6519ab6.html (archived at https://perma.cc/2QZW-MFCF)

8   Bloomberg News (2018) 'Why digitally native brands keep opening physical stores', *Digital Commerce 360*, 22 October. www.digitalcommerce360.com/2018/10/22/digitally-native-brands-are-opening-more-physical-locations/ (archived at https://perma.cc/XHA6-58SJ)

9   Arthur, W.B., Andreessen, M., and Chokshi, S. (2018) 'Network effects, origin stories, and the evolution of tech'. future.com/podcasts/network-effects-increasing-returns-trends/ (archived at https://perma.cc/VBT3-2XLX)

10   Choudary, S. and Bonchek, M. (2013) 'Three elements of a successful platform strategy', *Harvard Business Review*, 12 January. hbr.org/2013/01/three-elements-of-a-successful-platform (archived at https://perma.cc/TVH9-HZVU)

11   Curtis, M. (2020) 'Fjord trends 2021', Accenture. www.accenture.com/_acnmedia/PDF-153/Accenture-Fjord-Trends-2021-Liquid-infrastructure-Video-Transcript.pdf (archived at https://perma.cc/KXC4-9H5P)

12   Benveniste, A. (2020) 'The $94 billion fitness industry is reinventing itself as Covid-19 spreads', *CNN Business*, 1 April. edition.cnn.com/2020/04/01/business/fitness-studios-coronavirus/index.html (archived at https://perma.cc/89R4-2XSV)

05

Honeycomb as a platform

As I started writing *Accelerated Digital Transformation*, I was in parallel thinking about some disruptive ideas on how books are traditionally written. In doing so, I took inspiration from the predominant, disruptive business model of the digital era that I described at length earlier – the platform business model. I have assembled the Honeycomb approach from two different perspectives, on two different planes. The first plane is the standard book writing perspective, whereby I share the Honeycomb approach and my experiences as the author (the pipeline business model). The second plane is to view the Honeycomb from the perspective of a platform, whereby I have orchestrated and assimilated the viewpoints and thoughts on the approach from six different external, independent experts (the platform business model).

The six perspectives are outlined in Figure 5.1.

I spent considerable time with the above experts to garner both their viewpoints as well as their experiences on key aspects of the approach described in this book. Specifically, the discussion was arranged around the following topics:

- What does digital disruption/transformation mean to you? What business outcomes should it achieve?

- How can legacy companies inculcate a deep sense of customer obsession/service/experience into their operating models?

FIGURE 5.1 Honeycomb from the perspective of the platform business model

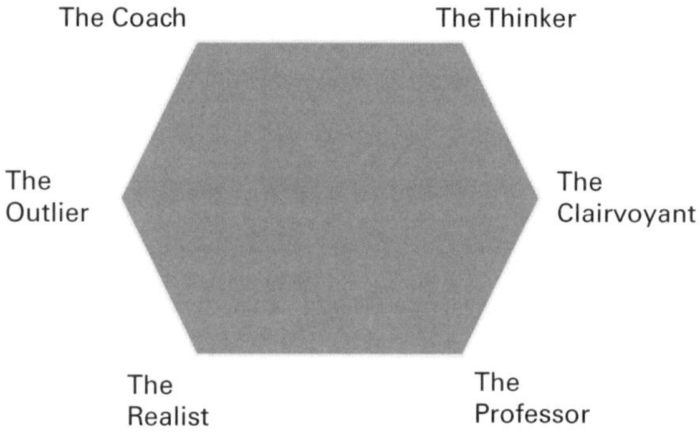

The Coach   The Thinker

The
Outlier   The
                                                   Clairvoyant

The   The
Realist   Professor

- Besides customer service, how should companies transform their back- and middle-office operations? What is the relevance of digital transformation to a company's operations?

- Is agile over-hyped? What are your views on the entire legacy company adopting agile ways of working, not just in IT but other business units? Is this essential for digital transformation?

- What about new business models? How can legacy enterprises find a way to evaluate and then launch new business models?

- What role does data and AI play in the digital transformation of large enterprises?

- How should enterprises set up an experimentation architecture to drive innovation and outside-in thinking?

- What are some of the attributes of a digital mindset and how do you see large enterprise embracing these attributes in their workforce?

I also wanted to encapsulate a full repertoire of perspectives to give readers a panoramic viewpoint on the topic of transformation. The experts have experiences from a wide geographical base – US, UK, Europe, India, the Middle East. In addition, they represent a wide spectrum of foundational experiences on transformation from the academic to being in the trenches and running transformation in large enterprises, to coaching leaders on the art of transformation, as encapsulated in the archetypes. Let me introduce the experts before we use this book as a platform and share their rich perspectives on the topic of transformation.

The Professor – Dr Stuart Evans is a Distinguished Service Professor at Carnegie Mellon University, Silicon Valley. Stuart's professional career spans across many areas of entrepreneurship, featuring extensive experience within the tech ecosystem of Silicon Valley. He has conducted research for SRI International and Stanford Graduate School of Business, consulted with Bain and Company, worked in investing for Sand Hill Venture Group, and served as executive management for Shugart Corporation, a Xerox subsidiary.

The Thinker – Michiel Boreel is the Global Chief Technology Officer of Sogeti, based in Amsterdam and is well known for his research on the impact of technology on society. Michiel has formulated the concept of 'un-organization', which lays down a framework for how incumbent enterprises should respond to the threat from digital natives.

The Clairvoyant – Paul Kinsinger had a long stint with the CIA, after which he was an executive educator at Thunderbird School of Global Management (where he is now an Emeritus Faculty member). Paul focuses on helping senior executives and their organizations understand how to navigate the challenges and opportunities posed by the powerful mega-trends driving today's fast-moving, highly disruptive, complex and ambiguous global business environment.

The Coach – Lee Ann has coached hundreds of Fortune 1000 leaders from over 50 countries to uncover their unique genius, bridge the divides that hold them back from transformative growth and accelerate positive impact in their leadership and lives.

The Outlier – Mittu Sridhara is a board level business and technology leader who has helped define, drive, scaleup and deliver four digital transformation journeys. His last transformation journey was with a scaleup, Careem, which was successfully sold to Uber for $3.1 billion.

The Realist – Radha Rajappa is presently the Executive Chairperson of a new age start-up, Flutura Decision Sciences and Analytics, and over the years has worked on strategy, market acceleration, value creation and in navigating the nuances of digital transformation.

Starting with The Clairvoyant, we will go through each of these roles in turn and share their perspectives.

Paul Kinsinger (the Clairvoyant) and Lee Ann (the Coach)

Paul

Most large enterprises, being asset and legacy heavy, are highly risk averse. Even in the pandemic, some companies have not embraced digital. I wonder how much of a burning platform must be out there before your executive pants catch fire! I am quite astonished by the fact that the pandemic has not driven more change. How can they continue to act as if this too shall pass? We read and hear about the need to focus on broader, more evolved shareholder perspectives, more open mindedness toward getting off the pure financial driven bottom line. However, I wonder where the real evidence of that is, except for the occasional outlier which all consultancies continue to flog. This remains the conundrum when it comes to true digital transformation of large enterprises. I do not think the whole concept of digital transformation is a myth. It is real, but perhaps real only for a small percentage of enlightened companies.

Lee Ann

We must learn as fast as the world is changing.

I think it is also a courage challenge, because you must shift from scalable efficiency to scalable learning. The former is characteristic of the industrial age as opposed to the exponential age, where the latter is more relevant – the industrial age with its large legacy structure, controlling, top-down mindset. Companies existed because it was cheaper, easier to co-ordinate within companies.

Now, however, we have leapfrogged into the exponential age. We were already hyper connected. We were already distributed and mobile and now we pretty much have all the elements of a participatory, distributed network economy. This pattern has accelerated due to the pandemic and the lockdowns and is not likely to slow down in the future.

Despite this progress in the distributed network models, the hard-wired attitude of 'we have to control and predict', 'we are going to forecast our way out of trouble', 'we need to have more meetings' and the old management mentality of perpetually chasing efficiency is still quite widespread. Someone showed me their mobile phone the other day and there were 25 meeting invites from a finance department in one week! We still try and predict, to put order to what is a completely chaotic world. The standard response to volatility is to do more and more and more – more efficiency, more predictability, more control – instead of stepping back and thinking about how we will create value in new ways in this changed world.

The mindset must shift away from efficiency to 'we have to learn as fast as the world is changing'. I think digital transformation is just one aspect of re-inventing what organizations are in the broader context of disruption and society. We must have organizational constructs which shift from mechanistic to more organic. And digital is the key accelerator for this overall shift. When large consulting houses talk about the power of transformation, the enterprise world translates it into digital business optimization.

Digital transformation is not about optimizing bits and bytes of your existing business models, but about re-inventing your strategy, system, structure, processes, i.e., your entire system of value creation. That is what disruption is.

Paul

In publicly held companies, the power still is in efficiency, in financial performance. What I continue to hear in companies I am talking with, despite all this, is that they have not let go – and neither have their boards – of the quarterly performance focus, and a very old fashioned and ruthless driver of performance.

My own experience has been that, during the pandemic, several service providers such as banks have cut people in their service functions, rather than ramping up their focus on the customer. They could have used the downtime to focus on their customer care functions. As a result, it has become even harder to get hold of service personnel. It feels as if large enterprises have missed an opportunity to ramp up their customer service focus during the pandemic.

Lee Ann

I see companies trying to infuse passion for customers into their culture. Let me relate this to a pharmaceutical company that we work with on what we call 'breakthrough customer experience'. In this context, it is not just patient experience, but also healthcare provider experience. Mostly, this distinction between different customers is not well understood within larger enterprises. One leader in the organization said that 'if you get the patient experience right, then the healthcare provider experience will fall into place'. This domino way of thinking is too linear. It misses out on key nuances in what a true breakthrough experience could mean to different customers, and completely misses the network effect.

What you need to do is follow the principle of really 'listening' closely to the customer points of friction. In doing so, you will realize that in certain aspects, these two experiences might be at odds with each other. In order to imbibe a true customer-centric approach, you need to think about each of those individualized, personalized experiences, then think about the flexibility and the participation that people want in their interactions, how to enable the democratization of idea-sharing through the customer journey, and all this should then translate into your service or your product.

One way we have approached customer centricity in legacy enterprises is by creating virtual listening labs, where we are listening to those that are closest to end customers – both patient and health care provider in this case. Consequently, we are excavating stories, which show where we have bright spots or pain points to provide value to the ultimate customer. As a result of these listening labs and harvesting these stories, we then try to extract out, through interactive sessions with executives and operational staff, what is getting in the way of providing value to the customers. Finally, mining of the data from these exercises yields the two or three mindsets which are causing the friction points in provision of exemplary customer service. These mindset issues can then be focused on and shifted.

Another interesting aspect is how we educate today. It is all about expertise, the degrees we hold and the knowledge we acquire, as opposed to starting with empathy. In my view, design thinking and digital transformation go hand-in-hand. Design thinking helps to start with thinking about the customer or people first and empathizing with their needs. Tech firms have firmly baked design thinking concepts into their product life cycles and this is one of the reasons they have done so well. We in the enterprise world need to bring that kind of thinking into everything we do. Sometimes people who have a certain number of degrees after their name, or who have a certain title, are very proud and focused on perfection versus the messiness of getting something out there, testing and experimenting and getting the learning as fast as you can. This kind of thinking is 180 degrees different and it is deeply uncomfortable for people. However, it is a critical need for the disruption agenda.

Paul

As legacy companies start to look at how they become more like disrupters, they have to learn to 'straddle' both worlds. They must do both things at once – keep their legacy businesses going, while at the same time starting up their new business and making it successful. And eventually they might even shift out of the legacy business into the new one.

I used to think that the biggest challenge in this would be to establish the new business model and find a way to let it flourish. I am beginning to realize that equal to that, and if not an even a bigger challenge, is the ability to look at the legacy side and deal with the sclerosis that impairs it. You have to bring the same exponential thinking mindset to internal processes and systems on the legacy side because it is only there so that you can free up resources to fund the new business. The need to exponentially impact the legacy side of the straddle to me is the biggest blind spot legacy companies face and is the thing that is holding them up the most.

Lee Ann

Tied with that is job security. Look at the impact of AI. Certain processes can be completely transformed with AI and companies should be making massive changes with the advent of AI. Better to do it now than any other time, during Covid, when we should be able to rip off the bandage. However, the legacy enterprise beliefs around employment, how to reallocate resources, and retraining people act as a deterrent to disruption.

Those firms that can adjust their people resources and move into the future of work faster are going to be much more agile and versatile. The domain of 'our ways of working' is quite intertwined with transformation. Until you unpack this and figure it out, you cannot innovate new processes and ensure they are adopted. Technology changes and change management go hand in hand – and inability to focus on the change management piece also contributes to the sclerosis in legacy enterprises.

Paul

Legacy companies wanting to get more to the digital disrupter side of things will typically launch a little lab, fence it off from internal budget battles, feed it, and protect it with different KPIs and so on. That is one of the strategies we know can work.

However, legacy company leaders also need to apply that same thinking internally. Why don't they identify an internal structure, system or process and launch a new initiative around it – give it different KPIs, allow people to think completely differently about how to drive it and throw everything up in the air – as opposed to what Lee Ann just described, where introduction of new tech like AI automatically means job cuts, which is a threat so why would we do that?! Who is going to pull that trigger?

Instead, why don't we come at it from an opening idea which says 'there will be no job cuts but at the same time, there will be a 50 per cent increase in performance. Now you guys figure out how to do that'?

Lee Ann

I do know of one smaller, global firm which did exactly that in a fairly traditional oil and gas services industry. At the beginning of Covid, they made the decision that 'we are going to do our very best to preserve all jobs this year. However, we are all going to take a pay cut, executives are going to take a higher percentage cut. This will help us avoid layoffs. However, we then want all your creativity and energy to reinvest into the business, to rethink our processes. Nothing is off the table. We need to rethink how we are doing business; we need to optimize our processes'. The president kept saying, 'I know there are exponential opportunities out there, I just cannot see them yet.' This firm not only optimized their existing business, but also launched an entirely new revenue stream in renewables through the pandemic. This is an exciting example of the art of possibility. Their culture is on fire, their people are all lit up, they are more motivated than ever and one of the keys to success was the leader.

The president had gotten really clear on who is and what he stands for as a leader. He needed this inner clarity to make those tough calls. He needed this inner clarity to have the courage to go in the opposing direction to the majority of his peers in the industry. I do really believe that it is the external and the internal both put together which make good ingredients for transformation.

Success of Agile as a transformation method depends upon the organization and how much they have truly integrated agile. In an oil and gas firm I worked for, they had it embedded as a subculture and language. In that firm, there was both a positive and negative impact. It initially got relegated as an IT thing rather than people understanding the underpinning mindset of agile. However, as those IT leaders advanced in their careers and took on different cross-functional leadership roles, they have been able to embed the way of thinking into other business areas. Interestingly though, they do not call it agile, as it has become somewhat of a cliché, with consultants using it often and nobody knowing what it actually means!

In firms that do not have agility embedded in their cultures, you will only get blank stares if you mention agile and it may not serve any purpose beyond IT. In my view, you need to position agile properly and ensure it produces something tangible. There is an optimization and a speed angle. I have seen successes of agile in pockets, but I have not seen a systemic organization transformation of this across a large enterprise. Where there is a great leader who is intuitive, does not get married to the language around it, but gets people into a new way of being, then I have seen success in this area. In any case I believe it must be called something else and not agile!

Paul

I have a caution around the use of the word. It has been overbaked and overused now. I get so tired of business catchphrases. I understand the value of having a short catchphrase which everyone can latch onto. On the other hand, it reminds me constantly of the lemming-like behaviour of executives. 'Oh, let us run from this phrase to that phrase! And we will also run off the cliff with it if it is current and popular.' And so, I personally stay away from a lot of those phrases and use a descriptor instead.

I agree with Lee Ann at the core of it. The only place I have seen agility and adaptability is in a Norwegian firm we worked with. They have been shaping their culture for several years and this allowed them to respond and integrate new ways of working as needed during Covid. A lot of this started for this firm during the 2008/9 financial crises. Their major markets' competitive landscapes changed dramatically. They saw it and used that as the burning platform to move. It was an existential crisis. This helped them embed new agile ways of working into their culture.

Lee Ann

This same Norwegian firm also aligned their reward and recognition mechanisms to be more focused on strategic partnerships and rapid experimentation. In my world of leadership development, I do not know of any competency models or assessments which cover these areas of agile, experimentation, strategic partnership well.

Competency models which can give an indication on if a leader is more looking at foresight and more oriented toward that scalable learning versus just operational efficiency. Typically, internal tools and mechanisms do not help in bringing these areas out. However, it is imperative that rewards and recognition frameworks in enterprises align with the need for these new ways of working including agile.

Paul

This comes back to what we talked about earlier – the ability for legacy enterprises to move away from just ruthless financial performance measurements. In my view, when it does happen, there are multiple possible triggers for the shift. Either the market is moving you off, or your board is moving you off, or one of the executives is taking the lead to broaden that perspective.

Disrupting business models from within large enterprises is not easy at all. One way we have seen it happen is through at least one extremely forceful, forward-looking, risk taking senior leader who consistently kept challenging the existing business model on a regular basis. I have personally experienced one such leader do this over a decade and a half! He has not always been listened to and the things he suggested have not always been picked up, but he has been consistent and relentless. There is that fearlessness and confidence that makes you want to take the risk with him. He has challenged the incumbent business model at the core, even asking questions like, 'What if we essentially put ourselves out of business to get into new businesses?' Almost that dramatically.

Lee Ann

I agree it takes a leader of that fortitude, gravitas and inner courage to be able to hold the question and then hold the space for the unknown. At Fujifilm former CEO Komori-san questioned whether the company was still an imaging company. He initially encountered silence. Can you imagine the frontline employees looking at one another, thinking, 'What do you mean we are no longer what we have been for decades and we do not know what we are becoming?!' However, Komori had the courage to say, 'I can tell you for sure that we are not going to be what we were going forward, but I do not know yet what we are going to evolve into.'

Some of the greatest leaders have had the courage to say something to the effect of, 'I do not know exactly what that future is, but I am comfortable with the unknown and we will get there together. We will create it together.' Again, there is a belief within these leaders that they can co-create in the face of the unknown versus needing certainty to guide us forward. In the case that Paul mentioned, this type of leadership is what allowed that renewables business to be born in the Norwegian firm.

Eventually, for this way of thinking to be scaled across industries, the disrupter–innovator leader archetype needs to be uncovered, nurtured and developed within enterprises. And then, if we can marry these emerging innovative leaders in management with a disrupter on the board to prompt exactly those existential questions, then real change can happen. I believe this dual approach of management plus board involvement is quite powerful and will help enterprises accelerate the real difficult journey of business model transformation.

The other thing which is a big barrier to change in enterprises is the amount of politics, which slows everything down. Of course, politics is a huge issue no matter what type of change you are trying to drive. But with the radical nature of disruption, the politics becomes almost at an international espionage level in some firms. Politics is another form of sclerosis in legacy companies.

Paul

Despite all these impediments, for this to work there must be a core belief that there is endless opportunity out there in the realm of transformation. No matter how bleak things might look, there is endless opportunity to reach for. Whether you are the executive or somebody in the line or customers, you need to be convinced about this idea of abundance of opportunity. Also, the belief that you can do it! If we just harness our internal capacity, we have unlimited potential to tackle that opportunity. If you drive that as your core thing, how you treat people must shift. Employees are assets with capacity – with unlimited capacity as opposed to unfortunate costs that we have to bear!

Lee Ann

Data, AI and experimentation is going to be integrated into the way businesses operate in the future. However, currently I do not see companies making this the regular way of doing business at the speed with which they need to, except perhaps in the tech industry where this seems to have become the norm. Outside of that, I do not see it as predominant yet. It goes back to the learning shift. If a learning mindset exists, it is easier for enterprises to integrate new practices that scan the external landscape, automatically leverage big data and reward experimentation.

Paul

I see AI and data as part of the exponential organization toolkit that legacy companies are not uploading fast enough. I just cannot help but chuckle when I listen to people in legacy organizations talk about how they are making their product 'smart' and want to offer data driven smart services to the market, but when I ask if they are using any of these smart services internally, I get blank stares!

I say back to them, 'Why would I buy this from you if you do not actually use it yourself? It is like trying to sell me a high-end sports car when you haven't actually driven one.' That is just fundamentally unsound and shows the disconnect between how legacy companies think and the market. Several of them are not actually living what they think they are selling.

On the experimentation architecture, I hear two kind of versions that work. One is setting something outside the regular system so that it is not so easily attackable by the usual corporate antibodies. You try to grow it there and hope it is going to deliver. Unfortunately, sometimes the expectation of timescales is just too fast, still driven by that quarterly milestone mindset instead of those associated with start-ups. But there is that path. A lot of the efforts in this category that I know of are definitely works in progress. Senior executives and board members are still looking at their watches and wondering when they are going to deliver.

Secondly there is the kind of internal 'let a thousand flowers bloom' mentality in which a certain group of interested, motivated employees are given certain latitude to play around and see what they come up with. Both these approaches work as long as these experiments are then scaled to value delivery.

Lee Ann

In a couple of cases when CDOs or their teams are leading through rapid experimentation or doing some trials, they can actually seem a little arrogant inside of the culture. We hear legacy managers saying things like, 'Oh, so and so thinks they know the way of the future. What about all the years of learning we have had?!' It is threatening to others. Again, this human psychology component needs to be factored in. I have seen a couple of cases where this is ascribed as arrogance; however, this is usually due to the deep insecurity which exists in the predominant culture.

For the leaders driving the disruption, sometimes with the exponential curve comes exponential impatience. Experimentation ironically could be an antidote to that impatience – in other words, moving quickly with an attitude of 'We may not have an ultimate fix here, but we are going to experiment and get some learning'. This positioning helps with alignment and patience. The barriers to anyone driving experimentation are not new. This has been the challenge for anyone who can see the future for time immemorial. Experimentation is a key capability for transformation, so positioning it well and then ensuring you are able to scale the results to value are what is key.

On the mindset front, I believe it is not just mindsets that make the difference in transformation. Rather, it is ways of thinking, ways of being, and ways of feeling that are all integrated together. And if you do not do those at an integrated level you do not get a sustainable shift. Why? Because most people have hardwired themselves into a finite signature by the age of 35 and even if they experiment with new ways of thinking, they will snap back to their old ways of being and their old behaviour.

It is the same thing in any kind of leadership development effort. You cannot just work at the cognitive level, you have to work at the cognitive, affective and somatic level to rewire the brain and body together. There is a lot of recent research in the neuroscience of change and somatic intelligence which shows that when you integrate head, heart and physiology that you have a greater chance of sustaining change.

However, as soon as you bring being and feeling into the picture, you are faced with a misconception which has been going on for years. It is the misconception that you have to lay on a psychoanalyst's sofa and explore what happened when you were four in order to transform! That is most certainly not the case.

Strategic leadership development efforts that retrain people's brains and help them to unlearn and then relearn are what unleash sustainable change. Then it is all about creating conditions in which leaders practise themselves into new ways of being. Leaders, especially at the top of the house, have to pursue this unlearning and then re-learning philosophy with rigor and discipline to institutionalize the change at a deeper level of the organization.

What also helps is being able to show some success stories when those mindset shifts happen. They have to be able to see common people do something uncommon. Spotlighting successes gets people wondering, 'Hmmm… If Pedro in purchasing can reinvent procurement, then how can we do that here?' Find some uncommon stories of success and share them widely – celebrate them. This helps remove common excuses for transformation.

Paul

On the tactical level, there may be another route for companies that are trying to transform. One of the firms we're familiar with chose to offload 20–25 per cent of their legacy businesses, either through selling off or shifting to a minority percentage ownership.

These decisions accelerated the transformation of their company not only by offloading less profitable business units, but also through shifting out people who were least likely to want to make the shift into the digital world. Many of these employees probably also got what they wanted as well, which is to continue doing what they had been doing.

At the same time as the firm entered into new businesses, they were able to bring in a further shift in employee mindset through new, fresh hires. At a more strategic level, with this shift, this firm went from a company having an extremely difficult time in hiring new young graduates, to one of the country's most attractive companies for young, up-and-coming people. Now that is a transformation! So, there are ways to think about this through business strategies and business models that can result in a win-win-win.

On a different level, I wonder whether acquiring a digital mindset and the shift in enterprises to embracing it isn't basically dependent on demographics; whether you have to exit the last of the non-digital natives out of the workforce and especially out of the leadership ranks in order for a true digital mindset to be embraced; whether companies have to become made up of millennials and generation Z workforce, who essentially are already inoculated to the impact of technology and new ways of working. By contrast, these same capabilities are having to be painstakingly adopted in companies still largely led by executives from the analogue age. I look at the world and there are countries with much younger demographics, such as India. One of India's great strengths over China is that it is a much more youthful country. So, will Indian companies make the digital shift earlier, for example? Perhaps not.

Or perhaps in the next 10-to-15-year timeframe, shifting to a digital mindset will become much easier and people will look back and wonder, 'Why were people arguing about that 20 years ago? This is like chewing gum!'

Hence, the mindset question, while critical to transformation, may well play itself out in the next several years via demographics and a predominant digital way of working will emerge.

The Professor: Dr Stuart Evans

We are in the midst of a huge crisis and it is going to be a while before we get out of it. The good news is – and perhaps this is a silver lining – that digital transformation has gathered momentum. I believe we are in the beginning of a really interesting phase of innovation reimagining the entire foundation of our enterprises.

Given the accelerated pace of technology adoption, especially in enterprise software, the role of the CIO has become critical. For instance, having to provision for everyone to work remotely because of Covid made IT central to business continuity. Everyone is in front of a screen and the traditional enterprise has been forced to digitize many manual processes. Many CIOs/CTOs were able to accomplish this in days, not months or years.

For digital native companies such as Airbnb and Uber, the fact that they were able to build systems from scratch gave them a different perspective on digital transformation. Many established companies did not have this luxury because of all the layers of legacy they had accumulated. I do not think digital transformation is a binary option for traditional enterprises. It is simply an evolutionary journey. A key difference is being able to easily access all data on every aspect of business operation. Many traditional companies did not have the technology to get data driven insights and even if they do, chances are the information sits in incompatible silos.

The need for contactless activity has driven significant change in the way people interact and consume. Retailers have adapted to these changes quite well. In some sense, the crisis has been the primary driver of adaptive behaviour to do things digitally. Now it is up to the CEO working hand in hand with their CIO to start redesigning enterprises from the ground up.

CEOs need to directly curate their technology stack. The role of the CIO has also become much more strategic and they are often involved in board level discussions. An enterprise exists to satisfy its customers, to serve its customers. The customers, however, are all digitally served now. So, you have to have that capability and not in some back office with a group of people who don't really understand business problems and only know tech stuff. The strategic value of digital acceleration is not ambiguous anymore. This makes decisive leadership even more critical.

The crisis has also shifted compute to the edge, having low latency connectivity so that machines can be connected together and using millimetric wave radios instead of WiFi to have direct connections in factories, ships and cargo warehouses. Necessity is the mother of invention. Instead of reinventing a raft of new technologies, the trend has been to recycle, repurpose and reuse what is already there. I believe we are in the first innings of the post transformation world.

Customer obsession

A passion for customer or customer obsession is fundamental in Silicon Valley. It is fundamental to every business and if that desire goes away, the business is in trouble. One of the endearing characteristics of Emiratis that always strikes a warm chord in my heart was this obsession with customer service and customer satisfaction.

However, like everything else, customer service should be reimagined as well. I believe what is going to drive customer service is data architecture. To get this right, a deep engagement with business domain experts will be a pre-requisite. Those who don't adapt will perish, those who continuously adapt will thrive. We call this forced adaptation.

You are also going to see the application of artificial intelligence (AI) and machine learning (ML) embedded in machine-to-machine interaction. Going forward, AI is much more fundamental to the way things operate.

When I teach my class on entrepreneurship, I tell my students creating a start-up is not about coming up with a good idea and a deck. It is about empathizing and understanding the pain a customer is experiencing in solving a particular problem. And so, I have developed a new Lighthouse Venturing conceptual framework that I taught in the Fall of 2020. It starts with identifying a significant customer problem. Early-stage start-ups are continuously learning and co-creating a standardized product (lightning in a bottle, as it has been humorously called). If it works, venture capitalists (VCs) pour rocket fuel on and scale up quickly. Getting that standardized product is really hard to do and the majority fail.

Then you create six or seven companies who share the data on that particular problem to discover the 'greatest common denominator'. It is not so much the obsession with the customer itself as it is about a desire to solve a very difficult problem that would be highly beneficial if it were to be solved. That is what Amazon has done so well solving customer problems at scale; it shows it can be done.

A consequence of working remotely is that there has been a flattening of hierarchies. When you used to have an 'all hands' meeting in a global firm, not everyone participated equally. Now everyone is experiencing the same environment in the same way, they can participate on an equal basis. I experience this with our students as well. When everyone is remote, it provides a common level of receptivity. CEOs now have the ability to align and realign the enterprise in a way that they couldn't do before. Hence, instead of having little pieces of transformation, or the old bi-modal approach, you can align the entire enterprise.

There is a range of things that CEOs have to deal with, from identifying changing customer needs, to building robust organizations that can get through a crisis. Another manifestation of the digital era are centres of excellence in different parts of the world. To leverage global capabilities, we are going to see the emergence of federated organizations. I prefer to call them nodal organizations, where you have certain clusters of domain experts making significant contributions based on their unique capabilities. Some CEOs are even saying, 'We don't need a HQ building. What we need are smaller modular units which can fit together, which are self-contained or can be easily mixed and matched as we need scale up or down when needs evolve.' I believe this is a fundamental shift in organizational structure. The C-suite does not have to be in a HQ anymore.

On agile, I believe it has had its time when it comes to the larger enterprise context. It was fashionable to deploy these agile methods in the go-go years of strong profitability. Does a CEO want their finance organization to be agile? Operations and safety need rigid protocols and procedures. It is really horses for courses. Agility is only one of the needed attributes. Equally important is the ability to be robust by having shock absorbers kick in quickly when you are about to hit a wall. You would not call the application of shock absorbers an agile process, but nonetheless they protect you from external threats.

Companies are redefining their value propositions with digital technology and this requires creative solutions. Flexibility is about doing things differently. When we have these growth periods, we think that things will be like this forever – clearly a fallacious view to hold. I am always stuck by this notion of what an English economist called 'kaleidoscopic change' when all the rules change at the same time. And the rules have all changed now. It should be obvious to everybody as we go through the Covid crisis that we are not going to go from one steady state to another. The new rules of the game are about surfing continuous waves of innovation and transformation.

The CEO's role is to be the chief salesperson, just as most entrepreneurs are. If you look at start-up companies, the co-founders are the chief evangelists early on. They are directly involved with tweaking and learning and seeing what can be done, experimenting to try and see what the range of potential solutions might be. Trust the evidence of your own eyes about what works and what does not work. You don't need to be a rocket scientist to figure out whether somebody is happy with what they have got. At the end of the day, you need to be delighting customers with what you do, the quality of your product and the desire to bring customers on the journey to liberate more value. And I think the role of the CIO in Silicon Valley has evolved along those lines. They become ambassadors, not just for the product itself, but also for the way that the business is run.

Almost every company will have to re-think their business model. It is not just about being disrupted by start-ups like Uber and Airbnb. That paranoia, though real at times, was the first phase of digital transformation. It has taken this crisis to show that even Uber's business model was not invincible. The ephemeral nature of business models is what CEOs have got to get used to, because no company is an island. It has to exist in an ecosystem. Evolving components and different players in the ecosystem adjust their business models and their interaction with customers. So, the value prop that you provide has to mirror the needs of the time. For example, Walmart is putting drive-in theatres by modifying their parking lots. Amazon is buying up shopping malls as distribution centres. So, you have to be creative when it comes to business models.

Schumpeter distinguished between an adaptive response, making incremental changes to existing business, from the creative response, which is much more the entrepreneurial approach. Right now, I believe the creative response is what CEOs of legacy enterprises need to focus on.

The Thinker: Michiel Boreel

Digital transformation is very situational; it depends on every individual organization. You see big differences between different organizations. In the end, it is about giving the customer what he/she wants as fast as you can possibly can. It is about obsessing with the customer.

That being said, I think that there is a shift now on what are table stakes and what is beyond. I am quite frustrated with the fact that too many organizations are still saying that the end goal of digital transformation is convenience. Convenience is a great goal, but it is too low a goal. Convenience is table stakes. Of course, it has to be convenient, but what are we delivering beyond convenience? That is where I spend a lot of time with our clients as well – discussing how you can reach higher.

Digital transformation is about the art of the possible. It is about reaching beyond for your customers. If I take a bank as an example, in the first phase of digital transformation they have just focused on how we can make it more convenient to make a payment or to do an investment or get an insurance offer, etc. This is fine as it was too cumbersome and difficult to do these basic things earlier. But that is not the only need people have nowadays. It is not only about doing a payment. It is about their financial future.

Hence, a goal which will reach beyond convenience is how can we as a bank become a guardian of the financial future of our clients, which is a much wider and much more far-reaching goal. That is the first thing I see.

The second thing in relation to this topic on which I am starting some thinking is as follows. When you think of digital transformation, we have arrived in the second era of the transformation. The first era, the first 20 years – let's say from 1995 to 2015 – you had a general-purpose technology called the internet and we spent 20 years adjusting our business to leveraging the internet to the fullest extent. We first had e-commerce, then e-business and then we looked at optimizing our supply chain, and then we started looking at the customer experience and we created wonderful digital experiences for customers and along that route very new business models arose. The whole cloud business, the social media business, the peer to peer sharing economy – these were all born in the first era.

In 2015, a new era started, as also suggested by Professor Marcus du Sautoy of the University of Oxford, post the defeat of the Go champion Lee Sedol by Alpha Go's AI model, which is widely deemed as a tipping point. The next age of digital transformation is about adjusting your business to the new general-purpose technology of AI. The next 20 years from 2015 to 2035 we will be working on integrating AI into everything we do. The challenge will be that, until now, it has been every organization's main goal to create efficient industrial hierarchies, creating collaboration between people. The next phase will be around creating organizations as an efficient means of creating collaboration between people and machines. That, I believe, will be the next step in digital transformation. Automate taking away tasks from people which machines can do better while not forgetting that there are many things where people are better than machines. Make sure we let machines do what they are good at and people do what they are good at.

There will be a huge shift in jobs. Jobs won't disappear, but occupations will. A call centre agent will be replaced by a chat bot for sure, but that does not mean you fire the call centre agent? Eighty per cent of the calls that you get as an airline, for instance, are fairly routine, but 20 per cent are exceptions and they need exceptional action, where the guidelines won't create a solution. To work on the 20 per cent will take much more time but if you solve those 20 per cent of problems, then the stickiness you create with the customers will be enormous. Then when someone calls the call centre with a complicated query around route changes in the middle of the itinerary, you can expect to get the unexpected but delightful response, 'Let me see what I can do.'

It will empower the call centre agent to actually do what needs to be done to actually solve the problem of the client, which, by the way, makes the job of the call centre agent much more interesting. It elevates the job and that is how you create a good situation both for the customer and the call centre agent. There will of course be some friction – you may need fewer people or better trained people; this will take a significant investment in training.

Disruption always comes from other companies being faster than you are. This need for building an organization that is able to innovate as fast as technology changes, that is still the challenge. How do you create an organization that is a combination between creativity, adaptiveness and also resilience? This is the triangle in which organizations need to be successful.

We have published a report on creative AI, which is quite fascinating, using machines not only to do repetitive tasks but using machine creativity to enhance people creativity to make better architects, to make better doctors, to make better lawyers, to enhance the intelligence of people by using more data, more insights. That is what I would say is the challenge.

What is the business outcome you should achieve? Well, it is the same thing – a differentiating offering. It is being able to ask a premium price for your product or service. We have seen over the years that the economy is shifting towards the more differentiating offerings. In the first wave, the economy was shifting to experiences, and in the second wave, I believe it is going from experiences to transformations. Let me give you an example of what I mean by transformations. Companies will be able to ask the highest price and be the most profitable if they can help their customers to become the person they always wanted to be. It is about enabling a personal transformation.

I got this idea of enabling personal transformation when I was talking to the COO of Whole Foods a couple of years ago. I was with him and his chief digital officer and we were having a conversation about digital transformation. Whole Foods is this beautiful supermarket, and they pride themselves on the organic foods product category. When you buy from Whole Foods, you know it is always sourced sustainably; it is organic, healthy for you; the food and vegetable department look fantastic. It is a great experience to visit their shops. They had a lot of autonomy in their business model. Gary Hamel used it as a poster child for the new way of organizing – much more autonomy, much more decentralized, creating responsibility at the lowest level of the organization, delegating decision power to that level. The person that was in charge of the food and vegetable department in a store in say Austin, Texas could source locally and decide who to get the vegetable and fruits from. This organic experience was definitely their differentiator at the beginning.

However, the other supermarkets soon responded. Now you see all the supermarkets have a bigger organic category than even Whole Foods has! And the new players to the organic game have the advantage of a very efficient supply chain. What you see now is that the original competitive advantage is becoming a competitive disadvantage, because Whole Foods are not differentiating anymore but they do have a less efficient supply chain. They were in trouble before the Amazon acquisition.

As my conversation progressed further on how Whole Foods could continue to differentiate, the chief digital officer asked me, 'How do I create a digital experience that is as good as visiting the store?' She quipped, 'You cannot pick an apple and look at it from all sides and feel it when it is digital.'

My response to her was, 'You are thinking this completely wrong! You are trying to replicate an instore experience and take it to the digital arena.' Then I explained, 'You think that the people come to the store for the experience in the store, and to a certain extent that is true. However, really why they buy at Whole Foods is that they believe that by buying at Whole Foods they can become a better person – become healthier, become more sustainably responsible, become basically a better version of themselves. To some extent you have a great experience, but there is a goal beyond that – Whole Foods helps me to transform into a better person. Because I buy at Whole Foods, I have a feeling that I am a better person!'

That is what I mean when I say that you should not only look at the experience, but aim beyond that to enable the personal transformation of your customers, then also think how you can support the same transformation in the digital arena. Then, you might create a totally different experience while still serving the higher goal of the transformation. Obviously, you need all the technology and all the data that you can get to understand almost at an individual level what the transformation means to you or to me or anybody else.

To create hyper personalized, digital experiences, you need advanced AI to create technologies such as synthetic media. There are some negative connotations of this, such as deep fakes, and they get a lot of attention. However, there is a positive use of synthetic media as well. For instance, there is a huge opportunity if I could use synthetic media to tailor every advertisement to the specific things that appeal to me as an individual, at a price which is feasible to my wallet. That is where I think technology can play a huge role.

I believe the key to imbibing a sense of customer obsession in enterprises is leveraging the individual strength of every person, every employee. Basically, it is about values. It is about instilling a clear sense in every individual who is working for you who they are working for, i.e., what they are trying to accomplish is making lives of their customers a little bit better. That should be the driving force.

I see some pretty promising initiatives. A year ago, this board of American companies published a doctrine about optimizing stakeholder value instead of just shareholder value. I see some promising signals that companies are starting to understand that you cannot be successful if you only serve your shareholder or your own wallet, you have to serve all the stakeholders. By doing so, you will also serve the interests of your investors. So, it has to be much more of a balanced approach.

And by the way, I believe that incumbent organizations have a much better chance of serving larger stakeholders than the digital natives. I am not impressed by the understanding of the digital giants and Facebook in particular. I am not impressed with their understating of doing good! They only act in their self-interest. They are totally not interested in you, or what their service actually means for political systems, or democratic systems or freedom. They have not thought about all this at all. They only think about maximizing their profits.

Coming back to the topic, how can companies create a deep sense of customer obsession? It is by empowering their people. That is the most important thing. Empower people to do upon others what they would like to be done upon them. If you consistently do what is right for the customers, by doing good we do extremely well. That is what I truly believe.

I believe that there is clear need for organizations to be very clear about their sense of purpose and the sense of the interest for the customer. Because if you don't, your customers will walk away, your employees will not want to work for you anymore, and your management will walk away.

The example that Neetan gave, about your CEO visiting the locations where the value is actually created, this has to do with observations skills. Most companies are focused on delivery skills. Ninety-five per cent of the effort is about delivery skills. The truly successful innovators, the leaders of those organizations, also develop strong discovery skills next to strong delivery skills. Just observe how people are consuming your service or product.

The second important thing is this skill of constantly asking 'why, why, why?' Steve Jobs was constantly asking the question, 'Why can't we do this?'; 'Why do all the phones look the same?'; 'Why do I need a little pen for my touch screen when I already have five fingers?'. Constantly challenge your organizations with the 'why' questions, like a five-year-old child would.

There is this quote from Satya Nadella where he says software companies respect innovation over tradition. I believe that is going to be true for more and more organizations. Is a bank more than a software system? That is an interesting question. Most CEOs of banks say they are really a big computer with a marble storefront. They start to understand that they should not say they are a 350-year-old bank. Nobody cares! Tradition is not respected anymore. How do you innovate? How do you make my life better? How do you become the guardian of my financial future? That is what people are interested in.

When it comes to back-office operation in the context of digital transformation, I was quite inspired with the 'radical automation' concept Neetan came up with almost two years ago. If you really think about it in terms of radical automation, you should basically say everything I do more than once, I automate. That's radical automation. So, I was quite inspired with your crazy statement, 'I want to automate 95 per cent of my back-office!' That is the thing. Why do we use people to do repetitive work? They are not very good at it. A machine is much better at doing repetitive work where you have clear constraints. Let us leverage people on the things that are not repetitive. That is what I like as a nice design principle when it comes to the back office.

We talked about this idea of creative, adaptive and resilient. How do you do that? I think it is by implementing platforms, practices and partners. You should look at your mid- and back-office and see if we can turn it into a platform. And then you have to immediately think about whether we need to own the platform ourselves or whether we deal with at as partners. When we have a really good platform, we should again ask if we can open it up through APIs to everybody else. If we have the best platform that exists as a back-office, then why then don't we make it available to all our competitors? It is very rarely that the competitive advantage comes from your back-office. Of course, it has to be extremely efficient. It should not deduct from the value that you create in the front office. In general, if it is not differentiating, which it rarely is, you should not obsess about owning it.

Many organizations still think that their competitive benefit is in the back office, which of course is never true. But many organizations are misguided. For instance, the back office of your airline versus another airline look pretty much the same. And think about it this way: when you start your own company tomorrow, what is the first thing you are going to look for? Are you going to look for SAP? No of course not! You are going to look for clients or customers. 'Can I create a fantastic experience or even a transformation for our customer?' is what you will ask first. Let us focus on that; all the rest is slowing you down.

When you are truly customer obsessed, it means you have to look at your organization from the outside-in. If you look at it from an individual consumer perspective, companies do not exist.

Organizations do not exist. There is no distinction between industries. There is a need. The need is that I want to be mobile. I want to get from place A to place B. All the industries that are involved in getting me from A to B, I am totally not interested in them. I understand there will be an ecosystem of many players, of many different industries that fulfil my need. What is interesting is that when you look at it that way, there are only a limited amount of needs that people have – probably 7–10 needs. Hence, there are probably only that many ecosystems that can exist. Of course, within the ecosystem you have many specialists. As a consumer, I am totally not interested in the back office that happens between this ecosystem. That should be invisible to me. I see my need and the way it is fulfilled; the rest is irrelevant and invisible.

I don't think agile is overhyped. I believe it is underhyped. We wrote a report a couple of years ago called the 'Un-organization'. Within this report we do a comparison between (a) the agile movement, (b) the lean start-up movement, which is more the marketing kind of approach, and (c) the management innovation movement.

When you look at the principles of all three movements, they are very similar. They use different words, but the drivers are exactly the same. It is about autonomy, it is about customer obsession, it is about delivering. In agile, the only thing that is valuable is code. You have to create stuff. Do not make PowerPoint slides, make code. The problems that many organizations have is that they focus on agile and forget about the management innovation that is required in tango. And if you are not willing to innovate your style of leadership, then agile will never work. You have to evolve these in parallel.

Successful organizations start with agile Dev Ops in IT; however, after around 2–3 years, companies realize that it is not enough. They can transform the IT function, but after a certain moment they hit significant barriers on the business side of the company. And then they start realizing that to become a truly agile, antifragile organization they need to evolve everything. Some of the most successful implementations of agile involve Biz-Dev-Ops. In those organizations, the IT department does not exist anymore and neither does marketing. They are completely fused with the business. They use different specialists, different experts and bring them together in an Agile team. They have their daily stand-up meeting, etc. and measure only the outcomes. They apply the agile principles across the organization.

Many organizations go into it the wrong way. They are not willing to change their leadership style from command and control to co-ordinate and cultivate. They are not willing to develop the leadership intelligences that are now required in the new age that is unpredictable and uncertain – the new age which demands not the standard strategic planning approach, but a much more experimental approach.

These attempts then fail. Then they blame Agile, that it did not deliver to its promise. But when you dig one spade deeper, they see that the reason it did not deliver is because they as management were not willing to change – To change practices, to change KPIs, to change the way they deal with organizations, with budgets, business reviews, and all that kind of nonsense.

I really think that the biggest challenge and the biggest disruption comes to organizations that are unable to change their management style. Management is the only thing that has not innovated in the last 150 years! We are still in this Taylorism way of managing hierarchies. While these worked very well in an industrial age, they work very badly in this new age of intelligence, data centricity and transformation. They just don't work in this age.

The problem is that it may take decades before organizations realize that the model does not work anymore. And by that time, you may be extinct. Nature's way of dealing with irrelevance is not transformation. It is creative destruction. Irrelevant organisms die and relevant ones flourish.

There are not many organizations that can fundamentally reinvent themselves. IBM is a famous example of a company that has reinvented themselves a couple of times. They are right in the middle of reinventing themselves all over again. I believe Microsoft has become pretty good at reinventing themselves over the last 5–6 years. I believe the main reason for that is the change of leadership from Steve Balmer to Satya Nadella. I think Satya did a tremendous, incredible job of reinventing a company of that size.

At a smaller scale, we have a client in Sweden, the Husqvarna Group, who are currently in the forestry and gardening business. What is interesting is that they are a company which is 350 years old! I visited them and they have a museum of their company history! They started with making swords 300 years ago. At a certain point in time, gunpowder was invented, so they transformed their company from making swords to making shotguns. They became a very important arms manufacturer. Then, in the 1800s, there were not enough wars, so they saw the demand for guns declining and hence they switched to bicycles. They used their core assets and competencies in metals to create bicycles, which was a completely different industry. Then from bicycles, they went to chainsaws. They are now going into automatic robotic lawn mowers. This is a company I quite admire. They were able to reinvent themselves not once, but consistently. And that is how you create a 350-year-old company.

One good trend, which helps companies reinvent business models from within, is that companies are hiring what I call technology knowledgeable business executives – The 30–40-year-old new age manager. Of course, they are an engineer or a business person, but they understand enough about technology that helps them to envision technology inspired business models. The way you transform your organization is by replacing your old guard with these young, tech savvy managers. Hire new management. I visited ING Bank and met their CIO Ron, who explained that this journey of agile transformation started in 2010. In the course of 10 years since the journey started, they have replaced 70 per cent of their management. From a generational perspective, that is going to happen anyhow. From that point of view, you could say that the biggest challenge of incumbent organizations is to survive the existing management, but there is hope, as eventually they will retire and be replaced!

Another challenge is that it is very rare that management would propose a successor that is completely different. That is why diversity become so important. You need to hire different people from the management that you have today. I believe that is a huge, huge challenge.

On the question of changing business models, I see that organizations struggle with that tremendously. All new business models start small as either proposed by someone in the executive boardroom, or an entrepreneur challenging the status quo outside the enterprise. In the initial years, the impact of these new business ideas is very limited when viewed from a profit and loss (P&L) perspective. The problem is that small P&L items are not on the radar screen of most managers. If you are managing a €20 billion company, you are looking for the next billion, you are not looking for the next million. However, there is a critical need to imbibe deep observation skills in leaders so that they can acutely observe and focus on small ideas, which have the potential to scale to significant business models in the future.

The other thing that companies struggle a lot with is corporate venture. The fashion used to be that innovation is happening in Silicon Valley, so we will open a lab there, we hire some nice people and rent a nice building along Highway 101 from San Francisco to San Jose, then we have a lab in the middle of where innovation is happening.

Well, they are closing these down after 5–6 fairly expensive years. The people in these labs are of course very smart and they did great things. However, now companies are finding out that the problem is not creating something at arm's length and creating some innovation at these labs, i.e., innovating at the periphery of the organization, but the problem is how to innovate at the core of the organization. How do you bring innovation back to the core of the organization?

The other problem with new business models is that, since we are so obsessed with KPIs and business reviews, legacy companies start to measure profitable growth much too early for their new business model initiatives. Look at how start-ups like Amazon became successful. The first time Bezos earned some money was 10 years after he came into play! He was focused on volume. He had different KPIs than a classical organization would have.

That is also my explanation for why innovation always comes from outside of the incumbents. And I do not know how to solve for that. Large incumbents are very bad at nurturing small innovation, scaling them into growth and then nurturing them into the next billion-dollar opportunity. One way the incumbents think about new business modes is that we will buy them by the time they become successful. The challenge with this thinking is that by then it is too late. Because you have this hypergrowth and as soon as the company takes off on this exponential curve, they are sometimes worth more than the incumbents. Airbnb used to be worth more than all the hotel companies combined. Even if Marriott wanted to buy Airbnb, they just could not. Hence, this old strategy that we can afford to focus on efficiency and operations and when there is a disruptive innovation let it happen and when it becomes mature, we acquire it, is very, very risky nowadays.

Navi Radjou shares a few interesting trends in new business models. He talks about micro manufacturing. From a sustainability point of view, why don't we take the factories much closer to where the demand is? Why do we ship all this stuff around the world? We could also create much smaller factories much closer to where the demand is. Hence, we will not waste all this energy on logistics. The other concept he came up with, which I find quite inspiring, is a business-to-business (B2B) sharing economy. It was in the last financial crisis in 2008 that Uber and Airbnb were formed, and they focused on under-utilized assets and making them available for everyone to buy/consume.

In this day and age, you have a number of underutilized assets within companies. Could you envisage a platform where you would make these assets available to anybody to leverage, in any way they want to? In many factories, they have equipment which is only utilized 20–30 per cent of the time. Why not make that available? Basically, that is how the cloud started, with the realization that you have this under-utilized data centre. We could look at many enterprise assets in the same way.

Data and AI has been the core of transformation already for a long time. It is all about data and it will continue. What is also a continuing trend is that data and insights are becoming very quickly the real differentiator. For instance, in the airline industry yield management is the most valuable part of an airline, which is all about data and insights. I believe that this will happen in any industry – that the data about the industry becomes more valuable than the industry itself!

AI of course is a term which is confusing. Advanced analytics and insights is perhaps a better word for it, in terms of the enterprise context. This will increasingly become the differentiating factor of successful companies. However, companies are very good at it. Companies are distracted in many ways. Most companies think about AI, but when they start with the project, the biggest problem is how to get their data house in order. They don't. They have the data, but they struggle with reaching it, refining it and then leveraging it.

Experimentation is taking the place of what strategic planning used to be. Strategic planning is very helpful in predicable industries. If you can predict how demand will develop in the next five years, then strategy is a great way of doing it. Now we are in an era where the only thing we know is that we know that our predictions are useless. We know that they will be wrong. So, if predictions don't work, then the only thing that works is experimentation. You have to try stuff. Try something, then measure what works and what does not and then you pivot. You focus on the things that work, you try to solve the things that don't work, and then you go into the next cycle. That is indeed the design thinking type of approach – focus on outside-in thinking and experimentation.

You need to have a very disciplined process on how you do experimentation. The experiments are constantly changing, but the way that you do the experiments, and how you measure the outcomes of the experiments, should stay the same. That is also why you need agility and resilience or robustness at the same time. The process should be robust, and the experiment should be very agile. The other thing is the importance of platforms. Many organizations think that experimentation has to do with invention. In fact, invention might also be the enemy of experimentation. You have to have a well understood, efficient platform on the top of which you can experiment. The whole idea of using platforms that help you experiment is key.

For instance, I have a constant debate with my colleagues on the Cloud where they think that the organizations are shifting to the cloud as it is a more efficient way of hosting. My view is that it may have started that way, but surely today it is not. Organizations are moving to the cloud because it gives them a platform to absorb new innovative technologies much faster. So, you experiment on the foundation of a robust platform.

To get a mindset shift, you need a burning platform, you need a clear reason for changing. And that is what we have also learnt from this crisis. I talk with companies constantly. The other day, I was talking to the CIO of the Dutch Navy. He explained to me that they had more transformation in a week than they had in the previous five years. They had a plan to roll out a system to work from home and the plan was for two years. They shifted everyone to remote work in a week! The power of a crisis to meltdown all the resistance to change is immense. If you are not in a crisis, then you have to create one. You have to create an existential crisis.

The Realist: Radha Rajaapa

Digital disruption and transformation stem from the fact that we as consumers who are buying products and using services have changed the way we work, the way we live, the way we sleep, the way we eat. Sometimes it seems like this change is only for the millennials or it is only for the younger generation; however, what I have seen over the years is that this change has touched everybody's life.

Just look at India. Look at a state like Tamil Nadu. If you go to the interiors, the way people consume entertainment, even the grandparents in their 70s and 80s, has completely transformed. They are now conversant with YouTube or over-the-top (OTT) platforms for their entertainment. With increasing nuclear families, globally dispersed, people are using mobile devices to connect and converse with each other. Every age has become familiar with these new devices and these new technological advances.

Devices, connectedness and all forms of 'digital' experiences are infused into all our day-to-day lives inseparably. Our attitude and sense of gratification has taken a rapid transformation! Every firm, B2B or business-to-customer (B2C) is finally embracing these realities of consumers. Hence, transformation is a must for every firm as they must serve these new realities of consumers in every way.

The new age firms and digital natives also bring a fresh perspective to the way they re-imagine how to serve the needs of the customer. Truly visionary and creative led innovations such as the iPod or the iPhone seriously impacted many industries altogether and altered means and ways of consumers experiencing music or using cameras, GPS devices, watches and many more. It is therefore imperative that legacy companies strive to sustain their leadership position or just strive to survive when their entire industry is being disrupted.

In a sense, legacy companies have no choice but to drive the transformational agenda in some way. This transformation is about survival, and it is about growth, but it is ultimately about your P&L.

I deal with some companies in the oil and gas segment, for instance, and you could relate them to traditional organizations. The upstream operations of exploration and production or the downstream operations such as refining have been operational for decades. But look at the pandemic and the resultant extreme volatility of the demand and prices that has had a huge impact on the industry. In addition, there is the perpetual element of geo-political changes which cause volatility. The oil and gas companies cannot stand still. They need to make their supply chains nimble. They need to make their production nimble. Which well-pads should be shut because they are not needed for now? There is an acute need for companies to proactively look at asset performance and reliability and draw upon assets and process optimization to bring the right efficiency. A geopolitical push which requires firms to focus on shale energy could mean a different strategy for the firm. The digital transformation topic is not only relevant to the fancy B2C world of retail and consumer goods or services, but also in heavy industries. So, B2B or B2B2C or B2C, the topic of transformation is an existential driver, to keep the P&L robust and continue to be an effective player in this space.

The disruption to our daily lives caused by the Covid-19 pandemic has even more deeply accentuated the need for transformation. I have seen this in other very established firms as well – in the consumer goods space, for instance. Our consumptions patterns have changed quite a bit, suddenly. In India, for example, all cities have local neighbourhood bakeries where people would buy locally produced bread, cookies and eatables for snacking, etc. And suddenly, with the pandemic, there is so much health-related fear that people have moved to packaged cookies available from known brands of established fast moving consumer goods (FMCG) players. For these brands, there has been a sudden surge in demand. Some of them had to set up new production facilities at speed to cope with the demand. If they did not, their competition would capitalize on it. Additionally, the flavours and the ways of distribution have changed quite a bit during this pandemic. I saw distribution related innovation from some of the very traditional legacy companies when they opened out their own ordering systems to allow access through popular messaging applications, for instance, directly to consumers and serviced through the mom-and-pop local outlets. The very last mile of delivery saw the use of push carts and bicycles in some parts of the emerging world! There was sudden demand in the market of a different kind and to capitalize on the opportunity, firms strongly and swiftly accelerated the digital journey during the pandemic.

The 'customer-in' culture

Having worked in digital transformation across different industries, I have seen many examples of enterprises imbibing a deep passion for customer into their culture. Let me illustrate with an example of a legacy company in the farm equipment sector, selling tractors and farm implements. Who is their end customer? It is the farmer. Traditionally, the distribution chain comprises of distributors, the dealers and then the sales staff who usually take the traditional journey cycle approach to selling through this chain. Also, agriculture is not industrialized all over the world and in emerging economies it is a native profession. Despite this traditional backdrop, the firm decided to transform their thinking and use technology to put the farmer at the centre of their approach to achieve their business objective of accelerating sales. They tried to understand and empathize with what would impact the farmer. It could be the weather, as it impacts the yield, which the farmer is most worried about. The nature of the soil also impacts yield. Pests have an adverse impact and hence the knowledge of pests and what to do ahead of time so that the crop does not get destroyed becomes critical. The type and quality of seeds is another important factor. Likewise, there are 50 or more parameters you can analyse which have an impact on yield and on the farmer's earnings.

Quite interestingly, the firm realized that there is also an impact on demand from the farmer's personal life stage and incidents. In emerging economies, for example, it could be the farmer's daughter's wedding and towards this defining event, they want to buy a new tractor. Milestones in their personal journeys could create demand for new equipment altogether.

The firm took the approach of treating the farmers as the consumers and personalizing the entire journey for them, as opposed to concentrating on a push approach through the distributor or dealers. This personalization approach was underpinned by technology, especially an AI engine which looked at multiple parameters, to guide the sales team to the best possible conversion possibilities and propensities. The platform also rendered this information in a systemic manner, which is important as otherwise, adoption and change does not happen. Traditionally, the firm would have taken the legacy approach of pushing the stocks to the distributor, building a relationship with them, and the distributor knows there is inventory sitting on their head, so they work on pushing stocks further out. Instead, the new approach is a pull from the true end-consumer and driven by a passion for serving a need that is stated or most often even tacit. The under-pinning AI engine recommends the leads to prioritize based on the propensity to buy. Rendering is done on an easy-to-use mobile platform which can be used either by the company's or the distrib-utor's sales team.

Collection and utilization of data is key for realizing any of the above. Most governments are enabling the collection and dissemi-nation of agriculture data in multiple forms because it is important to them as their economies are still agriculture dependent to a great extent. This provides one important source for the data required. The types of data include weather data, what types of seeds you should sow, farm inputs, etc. However, for the above scenario, it was also important to capture the farmer's individual personal life data.

Certain innovative ideas are feasible today – with new age AI-driven technologies – that would really drive convenience and hence adoption. As you can imagine, expecting the sales teams who interface with the farmers or indeed the farmers themselves to key in any data into the system will likely face resistance to adoption. One way to use an innovative technology intervention to solve this challenge is to automatically interpret the voice conversations that the sellers have with the farmers using AI (of course, with necessary consent!). The textual input translated from voice conversations can provide the necessary insights for the recommendation engine to use. This makes adoption so much easier and the transformation 'real'.

I find in the above scenario that the thinking was vastly differ-ent and highly customer centric. They focused on the life of the farmer in what was traditionally a B2B context and obsessed about the needs of the end consumer. Such examples of customer obsession are increasingly prevalent across all industries and a key tenet of digital transformation.

'Customer-in' culture is all about looking at the market and the business from the customer perspective and has the potential to unveil tacit demands. This is not only a big accelerator for business growth, but more importantly establishes customer intimacy for a lifetime.

The 'experience' fructifies when the promise is fulfilled

I often say to enterprises that whatever promises you make at the front-end, however much you work with the experience layer, you must deliver them through your operational effectiveness. You can visualize this as follows. Say, Amazon promises as part of their Prime service to deliver something within three hours. They will need enormous digital technologies at the back end to deliver to this promise. It would need enormous data churning at every point of their supply chain and back-end operations.

In a similar context, I was associated with a leading sportswear company who have been in the business for many decades. Sportwear buying was previously driven more by functional needs, whether it be for the footwear or for sports attire for the gym or for any other sport, but now it has become a lifestyle product. It is not just about the functionality; sportswear is also about your choices, about making a statement, about your lifestyle in general. Hence, the number of designs, the patterns have exploded exponentially. Initially, the lead time for the firm, from 'concept to shelf' or 'idea to store', was 12–18 months for many of their brands. In the years 2014–16, several newcomers came into this market. These were not only digital natives, but since they were new to the market, they were more agile and started bringing new designs and innovations to the stores much faster. They also ran their business at a much lower cost base. The designs started changing in the stores in weeks – 7–8 weeks initially and then dropping to 3–4 weeks.

Given this competitive pressure and changing market dynamic, the incumbent sportwear company had to shift their lead time from 12–18 months to 45 days for some of their categories! This clearly needed a significant transformation to the back-end operations of the business, including their supply chain, the suppliers and design teams. They shifted from the traditional base of design to a collaborative design model. They brought in their consumers, athletes, freelance designers in a collaborative process with their design teams. They realized that their own design teams sitting in a cosy corner and designing on behalf of the customers would not be able churn these new designs out at the pace required. They would also not be able to capture the right consumer sentiment.

Personally, I am an avid shopper and I believe shopping is both a cognitive and an emotional experience. You do look for value and functionality, but then there is also an amount of emotion which goes into what appeals to you. Hence, this company had to bring these emotional elements into the design though this collaborative process. It is not easy to change from the traditional operating model to a collaborative one. For instance, it needs a deep culture change to accept that a freelancer can contribute equally. Additionally, products needed to cater to specific consumer needs in their design. For instance, some consumers wanted their sportswear in florescent, shiny, which the company had never done before! Hence, this change is not easy at all. However, changes had to be made. There was no way out and the key area of transformation was in the entire back office.

Besides these individual transformations in the back-end processes, there is also a critical need to integrate all the processes to deliver the promise being made to the customer – from design to supply, to where to source globally. In some cases, they had to shift their production and localize, because if you are manufacturing in Asia, and you are taking products across the globe, it could be six weeks from the time you manufacture to deliver it to the stores. So, several processes had to be integrated at the back-end to achieve this lead time reduction, right from marketing to the supply chain to production and design.

Typically, people used to talk about digital transformation first at the front-end. It was all about creative content, e-commerce, conversational bots, personalization and running AI driven campaigns. However, especially during the pandemic, there has been increased stress on operations for digital transformation, transforming factories towards autonomous operations. You must bring extreme agility, cost savings, energy savings to your production lines to contain cost during hard times and to meet the varying demand. Also, the pandemic has resulted in extreme volatility in sales and you do not really know what is going to sell now. Hence, production facilities must change in many ways. First, in terms of cost. When the demand for a particular category decreases significantly, how do you reduce cost of production? Which equipment do you use, which do you shut down, and when? How do you optimize the production line for some other product for which the demand has surged?

Organizations are now utilizing predictive technologies and AI, which were earlier used only for monitoring, to optimize the back office and production lines. People involved in the back end are also of a completely different persona. They are different from marketers or sales staff. They need to be taken along in this journey, educating them that these technologies are not being deployed to replace them but to augment them and help the company become agile to serve the new age consumers. The operations and back-office transformation which was an after-thought or a deferred step of the digital journey is clearly seeing massive need and focus for change.

Agility with a small 'a'

Agile first started with the software field. I believe it was initially not highly successful, as agile is not just about setting up pods for delivery, but it is about technology and business teams really working together. It has its own challenges, but I am a big supporter of agile as I strongly believe what you need across the company is agility and nimbleness. It is not about software, but more about the decision-making the company does. When you buy a product on Amazon and you want to return it, the front-end person at Amazon is empowered and equipped to make that decision with the right system support. This agility underpinned by empowerment is important to all the functions within an enterprise. If you do not practice it across the company, your decision-making ability at the various moments of truth of your customers is going to reduce.

I worked for Microsoft, which was an Office and Windows company for decades. It transformed to a most-valued Cloud and AI company. For a behemoth like that, with the engineering teams being so pivotal and powerful, how do they change the culture, to make it agile, to transform it in such a profound way? It is not easy, but as Microsoft showed, it can be done with extreme dedication to the ultimate purpose and to the process. Today, even in a corner in India, for example, if there is a genuine need and you are prioritizing to serve that need from the customers, it goes straight back to the engineering teams for innovation. The need for agility is not only at the front-end and in operations, but also at the core of product or service innovation and that keeps the firm ahead amidst a constantly changing and evolving market.

Agility with a big 'A' is what the consultants flog, but what I feel is important is organizational agility with a small 'a', which is about nimbleness, responsiveness and ability to respond to changing dynamics fast and in a systemic manner.

Does transformation always mean disrupting your business model?

When incumbents think about new business models, they immediately look at the digital natives. For example, if you are in the car business, you immediately think about Uber and start working out business models which copy the digital natives, such as ride share. Do you always need to disrupt all you have and move to an altogether different model? This is neither easy nor recommended in my opinion.

An interesting example I experienced on this subject was with a company in the US which was in the parts supply business. They were looking at maintenance repair overhaul (MRO) items such as tooling equipment, safety gloves, etc. They were not into the critical bill of material (BOM) parts, but MRO items such as the above. It was a family company with many generations leading and being a market leader in this domain. In their operations, they used to have something they called the Big Book, which was a catalogue of 500,000 odd MRO items. This would sit on every factory floor and workers would use it to replenish their items. This company was doing simply fine until the time Amazon arrived!

The executives became worried that if Amazon ventured into the parts supply business, they would get wiped out. Given this threat, they had to re-imagine their business. Despite being family owned, they were forward-looking, so around 2015 they started thinking about how they could disrupt themselves and their business model.

However, to ideate about how to disrupt your business is never easy. There is plethora of ideation techniques that are available and you need to choose what works for you. One that I have seen work well is a simple process of randomly picking two entities or words that are relevant to the business and ideating in a group to bring some forced association or connections to generate inspiring ideas. In this context, looking at 'parts' and 'customer' as two entities and encouraging the team to come out with many possibilities and then connecting with the larger vision of business is both fun and brings forth awe-inspiring ideas.

Another method is to run many smaller innovations and experiments to try out different aspects of a new business model and slowly something new will emerge. The parts supplier company changed to a majority e-commerce business model from the big book paradigm which existed earlier.

In my experience, while transforming business models is difficult, it is possible. An existential threat from a digital native helps by creating a burning platform. Engaging the workforce in ideation sessions using some unique techniques to bring out business model related ideas helps as well. I believe you do not always need to suddenly morph into a new business model just because there is a trigger. This journey is much more organic and evolutionary in nature.

There is no transformation without effective use of data

I am a big fan of effective, thoughtful, meaningful and ethical use of data. I feel that in any programme of change, if you really want to look at differentiation in your firm, you want to look at acceleration, you want to look at leadership, conquer competition, or go up the ladder in multiple points in your industry, then data is essential. There is no transformation without effective use of data.

For all the successful e-commerce experiences for consumers, and the supply chain that enables fulfilment of that experience, the underpinning enabling capability is data. Data has a definitive stamp on every aspect of the enterprise. For you to take decisions across the firm effectively, for you to find who your customer is, for you to deliver continuous innovation to your customers, there are limitless possibilities. You do not bring a step transformation or change in impact by just automating or changing machinery or processes in your factories. Collecting data and analysing helps with decision-making, but the most effective and impactful step to transform and be more agile is to have a rigorous feedback loop that brings on-demand, informed decision-making and ahead-of-time predictive controlled processes.

We talk about personalization today as 'n' is equal to one – every consumer is one unique entity, and you know that consumer individually and serve their personal needs. To make this possible requires effective processing of massive data. A perfect golden batch in a production scenario also depends on data. How can you make sustainable products that can establish the trust with the customer is critical in today's world? The lifetime value of your relationship depends a lot upon this trust, which in turn is dictated by the sustainable actions you take. All this is pinned on effective data that can help you bring radical transparency in your operations, be it ethical sourcing or farm-to-fork in the case of edible items.

Data has massive power, but it depends upon how well you use it and the veracity of data also becomes important. Taking in social data and all other different forms of data and creating your data lake is an established way to do this. Use it as a powerful lever with a functional and a market or customer purpose in mind, just like the farmer data usage I spoke about. Means to drive your enterprise value up using the data is what leadership needs to think about and execute on. 'Data is critical. Ignore it at your own peril' is often said.

The sportswear example I used earlier is served all through by data. Whether it is consumer insights you are bringing in through your digital channels or collaboration or the transparency and agility in the distribution chain, all of it is about data. A global CPG major, early on, had a unique leadership practice. The firm had rooms set up for teams to listen into customer complaint calls. The senior leaders made it a practice to periodically put on a headset for an hour and listen in to customer complaints recorded in their call centres. This helped the leadership understand the consumer mindset better. This is another way in which data, in this case customer complaints, are used to drive a better understanding and feel for customer needs in the leadership echelons.

Data is not just about digital channel. In every form of experiences and touch points, data is constantly playing in our gut as well as in our algorithms to make the right decisions! It is not all about systems and technology alone, the 'feel' and the 'gut' ultimately matter a lot.

The deepest point to remember about data is to respect the privacy, to abide by confidentially and, most importantly, to use it ethically for social development and good. It should not become a weapon for destruction and division of our social fabric and communities.

How do we make it real?

Curiosity is a key enabler of digital transformation, besides of course leadership commitment. There is so much going on in the world. In every field of science, nature and in human behaviour, change is the only norm. Whether it is in material science or medical sciences, or just in the way humans perform their jobs or build their aspirations, change is the norm. Hence, it is important for leaders to be first curious, to observe, to see and then play it back to their own enterprise, employees, to their customers and sense how they can collectively think differently.

For an enterprise, experimentation as an organizational capability is highly impactful toward digital transformation. I found that gamification can help employees think differently. Your employees know your business, your products and your customers the best, so engaging them in thinking differently is essential. Because technologies are changing so fast, you can also get external help and partners to help with the experimentation. Set up a cross-functional team. Select some employees from technology, some from business functions and some who are especially creative people, bring in designers, some unrelated to your core business. Get them together and ask them to conduct experiments. This will go a long way in not only nurturing new ideas, but also spreading curiosity among the larger workforces. However, be mindful that once your experimentation and proof of concept is done, you need to move to a diligent process to scale and deliver value. Otherwise, you will be only wasting your time ideating and not delivering value.

Ideas need to be executed on the ground as that is the toughest part of digital transformation – making it real.

From a mindset perspective, curiosity is important to unlock different possibilities and different ideas. There are a couple of other mindset attributes which I believe are also especially important. Taking your entire team along and ensuring collaborative effort across the enterprise is where success comes from.

In my opinion, if there is one aspect which is the make or break in realizing value, then it is 'resilience in execution' – tireless execution and resilience to stay with it. There will be a few failures, there will be stakeholders who are not excited about the idea. Even in the leadership team, not everybody will align. Staying with the transformation, with the end purpose in mind, being agile enough to change some decisions in the process if required, but overall being resilient, is key to get transformation delivered.

There is also no shortcut to careful planning and execution. Though digital is deemed as very agile, we should not get carried away with this. Planning needs to be equally concrete, ensuring a rhythm of review, making changes to the plan if needed but in a structured manner. Resilience also calls for educating people, making them aware, making them see the value in their own small world. Work with the HR team to drive mindset change by not forcing it as a top-down mandate but making employees realize in their own day-to-day jobs how it will add value. A lot of patience is key. There is also a need to paint the big picture and show how the transformation outcomes will impact everyone. If the firm exists, the employees exist; if the firm grows, they grow; if the firm does well, it is accolades for the employees and all stakeholders as well.

Drawing out different 'persona' clusters of the employees and looking at the cultural change with a view of what it means to each of this persona is critical to draw out an effective change management plan (a cultural change done from the eyes of the employee persona you are handling), not a top-down view where you announce that you know what this digital transformation is from a market perspective. These are the five things to be done, and this is how we will change things!

It is about keeping people at the centre and designing those little experiments that help them realize the value the transformation will unleash. The organization and all stakeholders cannot be treated as one entity and one message does not fit all. Beyond the uber purpose and impact, bringing forth the value and benefit for every type of persona is key. If we can bring in a compelling sense of 'individual purpose' beyond the organizational purpose, the transformation will be done with great success.

It is about changing the smell of the place, to get everyone curious enough, to get everyone engaged, to get everyone to understand the value so that they themselves say 'YES, I want to move forward with the company in this journey of transformation.'

Curiosity, passion, compelling sense of purpose, and resilience to execute and to stay the course with the hearts and minds of our people brings the right transformation.

The Outlier: Mittu Sridhara

For me, at the heart of it, digital transformation is the ability to make people's lives that bit simpler, that bit more convenient – to create new opportunities and/or to create different opportunities through the digitization of the customer experience and the business itself. This opportunity is available to the humble incumbents as much as to digital natives. There is a customer need waiting to be solved, be it B2B or B2C. The other very meaningful opportunity is to create a new institution out of the old, where you enable the creation and growth of new digital skills for your colleagues. Create an institution that matters! In essence, this is what digital transformation is – making customer lives easier, simpler, better and creating opportunities for people within organizations doing that.

The third dimension of digital transformation is the ability and need to build a digital ecosystem, wherein you incorporate other players in the delivery of services to your customers. The good news in a digital ecosystem is that everybody benefits. The legacy enterprise, the humble incumbent, needs to orchestrate other players beyond their own services to deliver the overall customer experience. Hence, the impact of transformation is much broader beyond the boundaries of the enterprise.

To illustrate the broader impact, let me take the Careem example. While we were trying to solve the transportation needs of over 27 million customers and creating interesting career opportunities for our colleagues, we were also orchestrating the captains and creating jobs for them. There was a larger societal impact and purpose to our mission. This larger purpose and mission is what makes people go above and beyond the financial reward. This is when you become truly innovative, when you become obsessed about solving the challenge at hand.

Customer obsession to me is about living the customer's lives, living their journeys, living individual moments in their journeys and then translating all that into the experience you are delivering. It is really about being there with the customer and understanding the nuances. I call it as not only understanding the molecules but also the atoms; not just understanding the customers' broader journeys but also the component parts of their needs, the individual moments which make up the journey, understanding what works and what does not. There is always something to be done better and we need to extract that out, relying on our deep passion for improving customers' lives.

Let us take TUI Travel plc as an example. TUI was a $24 billion annual turnover company which owned everything from the airline, through to the travel agencies, to the transport companies which picked you up at the airport and the hotel where you stayed. Imagine you are a Scandinavian mother sitting in Stockholm in the middle of winter, where you get only four hours of sunlight in a day and you are obsessing about how you are going to take the family for a holiday. You decide you want to go to an island in Thailand and not to the city. You have two young children. You need to take three flights to get you there. You need to find the right hotel so that you can take care of your child who is lactose intolerant. The holiday is important for you and the family, so you take time off, put all of this together using the likes of Booking.com or Expedia, get it all sorted for December and when the date arrives, all of you are enthusiastically ready to take off.

Well, as it happens, your flight gets delayed, your ground transport does not arrive, you find a way to make it to the hotel, which does not at all look like what you saw online, and your child falls ill as they did not fix the food properly for them! You carry on and have your holiday; however, it was a lot of hassle and the experience leaves a bad taste and memory.

Now, let's re-imagine this same journey but done through a customer-obsessed mindset and business model. This, by the way, is what we did around seven years ago when I was the digital and

IT head at TUI. This re-imagined customer journey was a key component of our digital transformation.

The same mother books her travel through TUI. We collect the family and their bags from home. The next time the family sees the bags is when they show up in their hotel room. Holidays are about creating memories for you and your families. We have a little app which helps you navigate through your entire journey, including helping you with what you can do during your holiday. It tells you about the destination, it has a planner, a count-down clock and a checklist of things you need to put into your luggage.

The app notices that Pernela (the mother) forgot to include sunscreen, which was there on her checklist. So, it prompts Pernela on whether she would prefer to buy a sunscreen and Pernela clicks yes. The family gets to the airport and the aircraft without any hassle. The airline is informed about the lactose intolerance requirement and hence food is served accordingly. And guess what is on their seat? The sunscreen lotion. As TUI owns the aircraft and the supply chain, it is able to efficiently manage the experience to produce this magical moment of delight for the customer. The family gets picked up without any hassle at the other end of the flight, are taken to the hotel and their room has been properly stocked with lactose free milk. Pernela does not have to go out on the very first day in a strange place to try and find lactose free milk! At the destination, the entire itinerary has been tailored based on what the family needs and enabled digitally through the app.

This is a story of how a traditional company can live the life of the customer, understand their needs and problems and then solve for them in the digital glue which binds the physical and digital worlds.

In the above example, TUI had a vertically integrated model. However, if you are not vertically integrated, then you need to do the same by orchestrating other partners in the ecosystem to deliver the same experience. Let's look at Careem. We started with one component of a customer's needs, i.e., ride hailing, but since we have over 27 million customers on the platform, we then got into the Super App pivot. We started orchestrating a much wider ecosystem. We expanded our horizon from getting you somewhere, to getting things to you, to food, to convenient payments because we have a million roaming ATMs in the form of our captains! This pivot was possible because it all began with this purpose of making our customer's lives easier, simpler, better.

Transforming operations is hugely important and fundamental to the overall digital transformation. Let's look at the TUI story again. When Pernela and her family arrive at the Thai island, they need to be picked up at the airport. The entire back-office operations chain needs to get data about the family's journey in real time so that it can respond to any changes that might happen along the way and the customer reps can meet Pernela at the gate when she arrives with her family. The customer rep who meets them has his/her own iPad app, which shows clearly who the family are, which hotel they are going to, information on the kids, their names and their preferences. The rep notices that Pernela had planned a local excursion for tomorrow in her checklist, which is not ideal given the weather. The rep can engage with her and offer her alternative days for the excursion and help change her itinerary. This level of personalization is only possible if due care and attention has been given to the digitization and transformation of the underpinning operational processes.

This process of improving and fine tuning the operational processes is continuous. You have to be at it forever, whether you are digital native or legacy enterprise. For example, at Careem, when we set up a city we found that it took us more colleagues on the ground than Uber did, because Uber had a lot more time to digitize their operational components, understand the nuances, standardize across different cities and build all of this into a digital platform. Careem had to learn this as they grew their business and focused on transforming their operations. Even the digital natives do not get this right from the get-go. This is about iterating and continuous improvement by living the customer experience each day.

Let me share another example from the perspective of a digital native, on why operations is so important. In the Careem context, if our captains don't make money operating on this platform, we are not serving them. For the captains to make money, they need to figure out where to position themselves to pick up a ride. They need to be close to where the action is. Hence, we have to give them the tools and the information to maximize their ability to pick up rides. These operational tools and dashboards for the captains were all AI enabled. We predicted when and where it was going to get busy, caught any drifts in the market by re-predicting in real time, and then shared this with our captains in a honeycomb-type heat map on their app showing where they were more likely to pick up a ride. The heatmap would basically say, 'Hey, Raheed. Today you are in slightly the wrong place. If you head two miles west you are probably getting a ride and the probability of optimizing your income is significantly higher'. This way you are not only driving personalization of experience for your customers, but also your operator and captains.

For a company to be customer obsessed it needs to be able to react quickly. To be able to produce a quick change in the customer experience, when you notice that something can be done better, the enterprise needs to be agile. The digital native is not necessarily better set up to be agile than the legacy enterprise. Yes, they are smaller in size and hence perhaps nimbler and perhaps not that caught up in the way things were done in the past. However, I had to embed agility in a digital native and the change journey was not much different from doing so in a legacy enterprise. Nevertheless, in both cases, agility is super important to allow the organization and its operational processes to react quicker to the signals it is receiving from the customer experience and tailoring how it goes about delivering the outcomes. Agility is important from all aspects – how an enterprise thinks about the customer problem and experience, how it experiments, how it budgets, how it measures outcomes – all of these need to speed up, become more responsive to change and customer needs.

Business model transformation from within large enterprises is not easy but definitely possible. It has to be driven in a very focused and concentrated manner. The entire board, the stakeholders, shareholders and management need to believe that it is truly beneficial to do so. I am going to link this back to the core, i.e., customer and customer experience. In the digital era, incumbents typically only deliver a part of the experience and rest is delivered through the larger ecosystem. If incumbents have to re-imagine the customer experience, then they either need to partner or merger and acquisition or aggregate into a platform the orchestration of that customer experience. It can be done; however, the organization needs to get comfortable with the fact that the boundaries of the experience being delivered are not wholly within its control. It is a new way of working. It is a new way of modelling revenue and risk and potentially a new way of making additional revenue.

In thinking about this topic of business model disruption, I was reflecting on the ownership structure of the enterprise. As an example, I have been part of family-owned large enterprise. In this case, the owner had the foresight to know that something had to be done about the business model. He was not clear what exactly was needed but saw the signals for change. Hence, he was willing to make the investments required and seek additional capital to begin building out a pivot for the business. Ultimately, it is about the leadership and stakeholder truly internalizing the fact that customer needs have changed, that customers are disrupting legacy enterprises, and that enterprises not only need to understand the customer but be obsessed about them. If that authentic leadership purpose and drive exists to serve the needs of customers, colleagues and partners then I believe the business model change naturally comes about, even in humble incumbents.

In my experience across digital natives like Hepsiburada (the Amazon of Turkey), Careem (the Uber of the Middle East) and humble incumbents like TUI, Ladbrokes and Sabre, we were digitizing individual components of the existing business processes to deliver the re-imagined customer experience. In both cases, AI and data as underpinning capabilities were not only important to transforming the constituent parts but also the entire experience as a whole. Use cases such as AI driven chatbots or AI powered anomaly detection in operations helped these enterprises digitize individual components of the customer experience and/or transform operational processes. You could do things quicker and better within these individual components with AI and data. However, since you are digitizing the entire experience, you also start to collect data between the process joins of one area – for instance in TUI the joins between airline ops and ground ops. This data can be used to sync up these business processes, use AI to drive the decisioning between these joins and thereby drive efficiencies, new sources of value and create competitive moats. Hence, AI and data have a profound impact not only in constituent parts of the enterprise but also help in transforming the whole both in terms of the end-to-end customer experience as well as enterprise value chains.

Taking the travel example, AI and data are applicable across the entire travel value chain. From search to ancillary recommendations during the shopping experience, to at-destination personalized itinerary builder, these are all AI and data driven experience enhancers. Also, AI has a similar impact in operations. Let us take a scenario in a hotel where there are 600 customers staying today. Based on their profiles, operational and external data like weather an AI model can model and we can anticipate the entire supply chain well ahead of time to predict what is likely to occur on that day. If parameters like temperature change on the day, then the scenario can be adjusted and the AI model can map out that the restaurant spreads are going to look like x and customer needs are going to look like y. How the scenario actually manifests in reality remains to be seen and that is when the feedback loop comes into play. However, depending upon your model and your data, you are going to get 80–90 per cent accuracy, which is a huge leap and value in operations.

Baking experimentation into this scenario, in order to improve the model, we can do some experiments (A/B testing) to under-stand better the customer responses to warmer and cooler days and how their needs evolve and use that to improve our model. You need to drive experimentation through the entire system to understand what nuances and personalization elements you need to give away and what creates conversion and/or greater adher-ence/stickiness and then scale those experiments into institutional capabilities at speed. From a culture perspective, you need to create a psychological safe environment where experimentation is OK. Failure is actually how you succeed. Hopefully, you don't fail too often, but you are expected to fail. And you use a differ-ent set of metrics. I call it an 'error budget'. You are allowed an error budget as you are expected to make mistakes.

From a mindset perspective, there are a few important attrib-utes which are critical. The culture and mindset of every individual within an organization should be actually caring and concerned about the ultimate customer experience that is being delivered. Individuals should not just be concerned about the experience they deliver and are responsible for, but the ultimate end-to-end customer experience. A culture which promotes collaboration across the organization in a very, very transparent way. Customer obsession, collaboration, radical transparency has to be part of the DNA of every colleague. The ability to understand the big bits of the customer experience, but then also break them down into granular parts. Having a language, a culture and a scorecard within the organization which allows seeing both the big picture and the granular parts is hugely important.

Another important aspect is creating this culture of continuous learning, of curiosity with the organization. Having that inquisitive mindset which says that, 'Hey, I heard this in the news yesterday, how can I apply it to our business?' or, 'That customer is doing this in a completely different industry and context. How can I learn from it and apply to our business?' This ability to continuously improve and knowing that staying still in today's world means you are dead! Having an experimental mindset to try something new, try something different, not just for the sake of trying but with a view to improving what could be delivered – being truly humble, hence I love the phrase 'humble incumbent'. We might not be the best at delivering everything, hence the need to be part of an ecosystem, to orchestrate, to collaborate and that collaborative mindset is also hugely important. Being humble in the cultural context is hugely important, as that is what keeps you curious.

Conclusion

As I finished these interviews with the six global archetypes and assimilated their varied experience and wisdom on digital transformation, it further strengthened my belief in the Honeycomb approach. All of them broadly align with the core tenets of the approach, especially the need for obsessing about the customer and using AI to make your operations invisible as well as connecting it to the promise being made to the customers; the need for data, AI, experimentation and agile methods to underpin your transformation effort; how business models change from within is difficult but still achievable; and finally, what lies below the iceberg and is the make or break for the transformation – the mindset, the culture, the values which run through the veins of the enterprise.

06

The Honeycomb hacks

As we begin the end of this journey through the Honeycomb, let me share with you some Honeycomb hacks. These hacks provide useful experiential nuggets of learning, which will act as useful guideposts in your journey. These should serve as transformation life hacks as you take your own, personalized journey of transformation and endeavour to achieve the promise of exponential performance in your respective context.

In keeping with the theme of tech-enabled disruption, I solicited the help of an AI bot to co-author some of the hacks with me. You will notice some amazing insights from my co-author and some equally amusing bloopers. The fact that AI has become so advanced that it can summarize some of the key learnings from the book so eloquently will further cement one of the critical tenets of the Honeycomb approach. We live in an era of disruptive technologies which have the potential to change the world. I have also included the blooper hacks created by the AI bot. This will bring out another important aspect and learning, i.e., technology alone will not transform anything. We need a co-creative effort between AI and humans to make disruption happen.

Honeycomb bot hacks, including bloopers!

- This book is about helping the industrial, legacy business models for success in the era of digital transformation.

- The exponential curve is the inspiration behind my belief that enterprise transformation using honeycomb disruption method will happen slowly first. Then suddenly, an upsurge in performance will emerge automatically, naturally, organically.

- Bigger the company, the bigger the work. The goal of this book is to tell the story of what drives the enterprise and its mission.

- My goal is to make life simple in a society where technology has become less about information and more about self-expression.

- My dream was to be a global ambassador of technology and innovation and an evangelist for the digitization, specifically.

- In a transformation journey best to follow the passion as opposed to just expertise or set norms.

- There is vital need to create momentum for the transformation within an inertia loving large enterprise.

- To disrupt, big businesses need to be at the forefront of getting the most out of their digital assets and having an entrepreneurial vision while doing so is the key to success.

- To disrupt the big business model the enterprise has to think beyond corporate capital. The entire enterprise has to think of where to go from here.

- To disrupt is to be disruptive. To achieve the goals of change is to be creative, to be able to push boundaries of what can be considered disruptive.

- Metamorphosis involves reinterpretation of the business model into a new form in the cloud and new business models being launched in a few lifetimes. [Can you believe this was totally conceived by AI?!]

- Transformation will not be an easy business to undertake but when it comes to providing a sustainable framework to address challenges of the future, it is important to build an understanding of the current and future realities.

- Businesses of tomorrow should be able to design and build their enterprises on the basis of the latest and best available resources. They want the tools they need to grow in real value, the skills they need to make profits, the entrepreneurial spirit they want to foster, as they build, create in their communities.

- The success of disruption is critical to a success of the business.

- A company will not only be able to take advantage of the increased market opportunities but will also of opportunities they can create. They must have a good understanding of the underlying business problems and tools they can use as well.

- Success requires a strong ability to change the paradigm and shift the culture.

And now the bloopers...

- The Honeycomb has bees moving in a straight line when it comes to moving away from the tarp or even going right when it comes to being able to do so. The bees seem to be unable to get rid of the tarp because when it flies.

- If you're in the market for a new car, you'll probably want to look elsewhere but if you're in the market for a new house, you may want to consider moving to Silicon Valley!

- The company is in the early stages of a major overhaul as it shifts away from legacy systems and toward a 'new digital' mindset. The company is in the 'disruptive phase' of the overhaul, which will include self-driving cars and artificial intelligence!

- When you're sitting there and taking a hard look at what the future of digitalization holds, it's hard not to want to get angry.

- The digital world is littered with images of cats and people on bikes, who are happy to get on and off one and always going to see their friends.

As you will notice, some of the hacks created by the AI perfectly summarize the key learnings of the book. However, the bloopers also highlight that that AI needs human co-creation to have meaningful, transformative effect. The A in AI is more augmented intelligence.

Honeycomb author hacks

- Frameworks are like good red wine. They add zero practical value when ensconced in a cask or bottle. They flourish when you get them out, smell those grapes and taste that pure magic on your expectant palate.

- There cannot be a panacea to digital transformation. However, there can be a better guide than sporadic exec tourism to Silicon Valley.

- How does one transform a legacy enterprise? Slowly first, and then suddenly.

- Larger enterprises equal inertia. As a first step, create internal momentum.

- If it ain't broken yet, break it.

- If you are a disrupter, internalize the three Ps – persistence, patience and passion.

- Transformation is not a short-term play. It is a long-term, deep haul.

- Sharp executives know when to rise beyond the limiting confines of their egos.

- In the digital era, only the paranoid about the customer survive.

- Transformation is not for the faint hearted.

- Alibaba.com: no longer just a platform, but a mini economy.

- As companies grow, they regress significantly on the collaboration vector.

- There are two types of resignations – resign in spirit, resign in body. The former is more dangerous.
- Agile with a small a is much more relevant to digital transformation than agile with a big A.
- Know to learn, rather than just learning to know.
- Capability eats credentials for lunch.
- When you get the right mindset, take care of them to take care of your transformation.
- So much value seeps through the crevices of organizational silos.
- There is no transformation without data and AI.
- Data has an options value.
- The art of talent management in the digital age is having the serenity to accept the heritage, courage to change the legacy and having the wisdom to know the difference.
- Cyber security and digital are like yin and yang. They need to be done together.
- Culture is a derived variable.
- Wins go viral.
- Platform business models are eating traditional pipeline models for lunch.
- If your pipeline has not been hit by a platform yet, it is only a matter of time.
- Platforms are the new engines of the digital era and technology is its fuel.
- Covid barged into the edifices of 'command and control' corporate architectures.
- Covid accelerated digital transformation across the globe.

Honeycomb platform hacks

- I wonder how much of a burning platform must be out there before executive pants catch fire?!
- We must learn as fast as the world is changing.
- We must shift from scalable efficiency to scalable learning.
- We must have organizational constructs which shift from mechanistic to more organic.
- To become a disrupter, legacy companies need to straddle both worlds – keep legacy business going and at the same time, launch new ones.
- I believe we are in the first innings of the post-transformation world.
- I do not think digital transformation is a binary option for traditional enterprises. It is simply an evolutionary journey.
- The strategic value of digital acceleration is not ambiguous anymore. This makes decisive leadership even more critical.
- Those who don't adapt will perish; those who continuously adapt will thrive. We call this forced adaptation.
- No company is an island; it has to exist in an ecosystem.
- Jobs won't disappear, but occupations will.
- The next wave of disruption will be about enabling customers' personal transformations.
- Empower people to do to others what they would like to be done to them.
- Nature's way of dealing with irrelevance is not transformation. It is creative destruction.

- Nine out of ten times when a platform introduces themselves into a pipeline industry, the platform wins!
- Ideas need to be executed on the ground, as that is the toughest part of digital transformation – making it real.
- Devices, connectedness and all forms of 'digital' experiences are infused into all our day-to-day lives inseparably.
- Transformation is about survival, and it is about growth, but it is ultimately about your P&L.
- The 'experience' fructifies when the promise is fulfilled.
- Shopping is both a cognitive and an emotional experience.
- In my experience, while transforming business models is difficult, it is possible.
- Curiosity is a key enabler of digital transformation.
- The make or break in realizing value is resilience in execution.
- There is no shortcut to careful planning and execution.

Conclusion

Frameworks are like good red wine. They add zero practical value when ensconced in a cask or bottle. They flourish when you get them out, smell those grapes and taste that pure magic on your expectant palate. That is what you should do once you finish reading *Accelerated Digital Transformation*. Take the key learnings from this book and apply them to craft and lead transformation journeys within your specific business contexts.

If you are at the very start of the journey wondering what to do, take inspiration from the story I shared in Chapter 1, *Breaking organizational inertia*. Apply a force to break the enterprise inertia using either risk or opportunity, rapidly build momentum relying on a good mix of outside-in and inside-out idea generation, and then do not make the mistake of leaping right after into execution, as most consultants may suggest. Ensure you take the key executives through an immersion phase, where they experience disruption with all their senses and not only through PowerPoint presentations.

Once you have built momentum, the execution phase is quite daunting. *Accelerated Digital Transformation* guides you to start the transformation journey one cell at a time. No big talks, no big bang, no big-budget allocations. Start the journey with an organization cell such as marketing, product, sales, customer service or supply chain and apply the Honeycomb approach of disrupting its six nodes and at every step build and strengthen underpinning digital capabilities. Remember the three key aspects of the Honeycomb approach as you take this journey of transformation. Digital transformation is what you do one cell at a time (the six nodes of the Honeycomb), what you leave behind for disruption to nurture forever (the digital capabilities), and what you become (the digital mindset, the transformed soul of the enterprise). Follow the Honeycomb approach to ensure all these three critical aspects are covered in your transformation journey.

And lastly, the Honeycomb hacks provide valuable experiential nuggets of learning, which will act as useful guideposts in your journey. When you are debating about the longevity of your business model, take inspiration from the Honeycomb hack '9 out of 10 times when a platform introduces themselves into a pipeline industry, the platform wins!'. Launch an experiment on how you can pivot to a platform business. When you think about how to impact your culture, take inspiration from the Honeycomb hack 'Culture is a derived variable'. You cannot change culture directly. Start doing things in a new way. A new culture will emerge by doing and not by saying.

There is no panacea to digital transformation, nor does sporadic digital tourism to Silicon Valley help. Each business context is different and unique. *Accelerated Digital Transformation* is an insider's guide to leading digital transformation. Armed with the key learnings from the Honeycomb approach, take a deep breath and leave the shores of your industrial era comfort zone. Get away from the sidelines and get into the arena of digital transformation. Roll up your sleeves and act on the first cell. With the Honeycomb by your side, I stand convinced that you will make an exponential impact to your existing performance, open up avenues for new digital business models and slowly but surely a mindset will emerge where transformation will be nurtured forever.

07

Reflections

I have been immersed in the digital agenda for almost three decades. In this chapter, I share my experiences and some of the key learnings at various stages of my professional journey. Overall, my career can be divided into three key phases, namely digital–transactional, digital–strategic and digital–transformational. Let us deep dive into each of these phases.

Digital–transactional

My experience during this phase was to deliver digital projects sharply focused on a specific business area or function. I believe most digital careers begin in this phase. There are several business domains; however, digital projects can broadly be classified as (a) third-party package selection and implementation for example enterprise resource planning (ERP) packages such as SAP and Oracle; (b) home grown or custom developed application implementation such as websites and apps; and (c) infrastructure projects, such as shifting an enterprise to the Cloud. There are also a number of operational jobs especially in infrastructure operations; however, my main experience has been largely in digital project delivery during this phase.

Bringing rigor to package implementations

In one of my first implementations of a mission critical airline crew management system, I realized that package implementations seem to lack the rigor and governance structures, even in large mature organizations. This was in the mid-90s, but even now, in 2022, I have encountered projects which are run loosely. My first professional stint was with one of the big management consultancies, about four plus years. One of the big takeaways from that experience was the rigor required to deliver large digital package selections and implementations, which these consultancies do a lot of. I remember being quite aghast at realizing that this crew management project was running without even a formal steering group in place. So, one of my first mantras in digital package implementation is to examine and then put a robust governance structure in place. Start with the basics – proper executive representation in the steering group across business and technology domains and then relevant line management representation in the working group. Appoint a proper project manager to manage the initiative and ensure there is a regular cadence to these governance structures. The second shocking realization is that even in large enterprises, these package implementations are deemed as a digital/technology project and business just does not want to get involved in them deeply. The general thinking is 'after all, there is an industry standard package, just implement it and we will use'. This mindset is quite widespread even today. The issue is that digital teams just do not spend the time and effort educating their business colleagues that package implementations and in fact all digital projects are significant business change programmes, and we need deep business engagement from the very start to go live and beyond. I was recently part of a huge ERP implementation of significant complexity. These projects have a propensity to go awry and significantly overshoot both timelines and cost budgets. However, this project went live broadly on time, met its cost budget and was celebrated across the conglomerate as a resounding success. Some of the key ingredients were an active steering group, comprising CEOs and CFOs from all group companies, a core group comprising key business managers from across all group companies, and relevant line functions such as finance, procurement, HR and of course a digital project manager who orchestrated a fairly complex stakeholder matrix. The level of working group engagement was almost daily and while there is no guarantee of success, in my experience putting these basics in place went a long way in a successful outcome for the project.

We ended up buying standard package solutions to automate business processes and then customizing them as if there is no tomorrow! When we are done, there is nothing standard about the standard package we bought. That is another key mantra: when it comes to package implementation, less is more for customizations. Ensure your digital teams are repeating this mantra again and again and again through the selection and implementation process. The steering group members also need to be primed beforehand and help to steer towards minimum customizations. There is one aspect of digital package selection and implementation that I have not been able to crack in my career. It's a bucket list item for me. There's an inordinate amount of time spent on certain package selections, where we typically send out a request for information (RFI) first, followed by a request for proposals (RFPs), and then go through a due diligence selection process before we can finalize the third-party digital package and the partner. This process for medium-to-large size packages is anywhere between 8 and 18 months long. There is absolutely no direct value accruing to the business during these months, except the learning which comes from being part of the process. However, this due diligence is deemed critical both from ensuring we get the right package which fits our business needs and, more importantly, to comply with a larger enterprise's myriad audit and compliance processes. The typical mindset of the various stakeholders involved with these long selection processes is to cover their backsides, so that tomorrow if there is an audit query, we can point to some documentation somewhere which explains that we followed the process to the T. I fully understand the need to conduct due diligence, but in a number of cases, we already know what we want, but just go through the process to cover compliance requirements. I have no idea how this paradox can be resolved. However, I do think it will really speed up the delivery of digital work programmes, if the speed and velocity of package selections can be dialed up significantly.

Moving away from on-premises software deployments

A key strategic shift which has happened in the third-party digital party architecture is the move away from on-premises software deployments to pay as you go, use/rent models, working off the cloud. This is a huge paradigm shift and digital as well as business teams should push towards adoption of this trend. The key thing to note, however, is that this shift is not just about the commercial model differences between license and software as a service (SAAS) deployments, a number of digital and business capabilities also need to align to this change. The financial model changes from CAPEX to Opex with this change, and that has an impact on the overall cost of IT/digital calculations. Hence, the CFO as well as the rest of the executive teams need to be informed about this upfront through a simulation, rather than see the change in numbers manifest, post-facto. The entire contracting process between license software and SAAS is quite different and needs education and change management across legal and procurement teams. SAAS forces a certain level of discipline to the release cycle and pre-empts too much customization, which is an excellent outcome, but it needs to be change managed with the business colleagues. There is also a significant change and investment required to fine-tune the cyber security architectures to support SAAS models. This needs to be planned well in advance of a move towards SAAS. So, in summary, the move to SAAS is good; however, the mantra is to manage the change rather than just let the change hit you haphazardly or abruptly.

Custom development software

There will always be the need for custom development software in enterprises. In my view, systems of customer engagement, such as websites and apps, need complete ownership and need to be custom developed. There is a need to take a strategic view of which digital applications need be used (software as a service) and which ones need to be custom developed. While this view is very dependent upon industry and specific company context, in general I believe that systems of engagement, systems of business integration and systems of intelligence represent differentiating capabilities for the business, and hence need to be custom developed.

The key mantra for custom developed software today is to 'reuse before you build'. At the start of my career, we would take down the requirements from the business users, then do system design, followed by coding and then implementation. While requirements and design are still key disciplines and need to be done, coding has now transformed more into assembly, rather than building everything from scratch. Those days of 100-member software teams, building digital software over two-year timeframes, is passé and dead. Ten is the new hundred when it comes to software team sizes and the mindset among your coders has to be about assembling components into a big whole, rather that writing all pieces of code organically. In the modern digital world of microservice and application programming interfaces (APIs), there are already world-class, robust, secure and deployed components available for most business functions, which can be assembled to form a customized software. There will be the need to write some business specific components by your coders; however, the method for that should be modular components, which can work and scale independently.

My projection for the future on custom development is a world which will be predominantly assembly based. I believe a new kind of app store will emerge where instead of user apps, various teams will contribute fully modular and independent software components as microservices to this new app store, and any team across the world can use these components to build a large whole, pretty much in the way apps are used across the world. This will result in a quantum collapse in both the time taken as well as the risk associated with large-scale custom developed digital software.

A special category of custom development, which has also gained significant prominence in the last decade or so, is website and app development. The early avatars of these digital assets were quite basic, content only. However, the real value to the business is when they transitioned into e-commerce engines, becoming predominant revenue channels as well as customer engagement platforms. In my view, enterprises should own these channels very closely and set up in-house capability to ensure their ongoing development. I have set up a few of these teams across multiple businesses. These teams are best organized using the agile framework for software development, as agile squads of between eight and ten team members per squad, fully responsible for a particular product, for example, an agile squad which develops end-to-end the airline check-in product. The squads comprise multi-disciplinary skills such as software engineers, analysts, quality assurance, solution architects. The agile method also recommends several ceremonies as part of the framework and while I did not force the adoption of all of them, some ceremonies like the daily stand-up are invaluable to ensure the cadence of these initiatives. The key challenge in setting up these agile squads is finding the talent with this modern mindset and then ensuring they follow a minimum set of agile methods and framework. My learning has been to ensure the due diligence at the start to get the right talent for this area, before going too deep into development.

On two occasions in my career, when I did a deep dive into the existing state of websites and apps for e-commerce, I realized that the architecture just did not support the scalability in revenue and commerce, which is a basic expectation today from these digital assets. Hence, I had to basically stop all investment in existing assets and convince the executives that we had to stop putting 'lipstick on a pig' and start the development of these channels from scratch. These decisions have been some of the toughest ones in my career, but I have strongly stood by them. The root cause of these decisions has been the architecture or edifice on which these e-commerce channels were built. I cannot emphasize enough the need for a rock solid, modular architecture to under-pin these e-commerce channels. Please ensure you get a top-notch solution architect to help lay down the overall website and app architecture before a single piece of code is written. The technology will evolve over time; however, the architecture needs to be robust from the start. If not, when you start scaling your e-commerce business, you will have no choice but to do a re-write.

The website and app developments are also unique because there is no end date for the project. You can imagine when digital teams go to the internal, enterprise governance bodies and say that there is no end date, the reaction that stimulates! However, it is critical that before commencing this initiative, the relevant senior stakeholders are engaged and educated on how e-commerce sites need continuous change and adaptation forever. These channels face off directly with end customers, whose needs are ever evolving. In addition, this world is perhaps one of the most volatile and subject to a constant flow of innovations. Hence, budget provisions need to be made to ensure that the channels are kept in tune with evolving customer needs. The way I have managed this is to create an extraordinary budget for the initial ramp-up period when you build the basic capability and launch, and then have a baseline budget and capacity post that ramp-up period which goes on forever. A cross-functional team of business and digital owners can then decide on behalf of the final customers which demand and feature to prioritize for which release, after the initial launch is done. The mantra for this type of custom development is to recognize upfront that this is a specialist type of project and ensure the above aspects of using the agile methodology, deploying specialist talent, budgets which enable continuous improvement, rapid cadence, and a cross-discipline portfolio group to prioritize demand into releases are institutionalized to ensure success of the initiative.

Infrastructure projects

Infrastructure projects are a specialist category within digital. From my experience, the technical domain expertise is invaluable for these projects, and you have to ensure that this capability exists from the start. One of the critical infrastructure programmes is the migration of the data centre infrastructure, which is most prevalent in large legacy enterprises, to the cloud. There is still much deliberation on whether we should or should not run this initiative. In my experience, this is an absolute no brainer and as digital leadership, this is something we should give impetus to. The mantra here is 'just do it'. No doubt, you will need to run a beauty contest among the hyperscalers; however, get a passionate infrastructure person, ideally someone who has run cloud migrations before, build a robust business case and then just get this one done. The hyperscalers more or less and sooner or later catch up with each other on the functional and technical features, so you won't go wrong in migrating to any one of them. The key is to ensure your infrastructure architecture is built in such a way that your cost of switching from one cloud provider to another is minimal. This gives you strategic leverage over the suppliers and helps keep the costs under control.

I have led at least three large-scale cloud transformations. There is a tendency to make too much hoo-ha about this initiative both within large enterprises as well as externally in technology media. The initiative is touted as the be-all of transformation. While I fully agree this is an important initiative, there is much more to digital transformation than a move to the cloud. Hence, my suggestion is to focus on the job at hand, do not spend too much time analysing, assemble a passionate team of experts, choose a partner among one of the hyerscalers, concentrate and get the job done. You will face a challenge in getting a positive business case and a reasonable payback period, so prepare for that challenge from your finance governance. The key challenge is to have a good handle on the state of your current data centres and the investment required in the future to ensure the infrastructure remains current and cyber security vulnerabilities are managed. In most cases, you will find that the business case will largely hinge on cost avoidance on investment in existing data centres. That is perfectly fine, as long as you have done the due diligence on your existing data centre infrastructure and done a good forecast of the investments required in the future.

One of the other key learnings was the need for strong governance once the move to the cloud has been consummated. I had personal experience of this, when after eight to nine months post our cloud migration, I was presented with a hefty bill of cloud consumption, not in line with the budgets. You can imagine the shock I got! Once you unleash the power of the cloud, it liberates people from the lead times and painful approval workflows of the erstwhile data centre paradigm. Anyone can boot up a server on the cloud with a few clicks. There are also a number of options available for innovation and experimentation, again available at a few clicks. This freedom needs to be managed. I later learned that the specific cloud discipline which helps manage this freedom is called FinOps. It is critical as part of the design of the move to the cloud, the project team take the relevant learnings from FinOps and institutionalize them within the enterprise. This will ensure the right balance between freedom and cost control and is critical to the ongoing success of your cloud transformation.

Hybrid transactional digital projects

A hybrid transactional digital project is developing and then implementing business intelligence within a large enterprise. This kind of project involves both a number of third-party components as well as a fair bit of custom development. There is a huge thirst for reporting and analytics within enterprises. My first experience was implementing from scratch the analytical tool set for an airline's operational division. There was a huge amount of effort which went into getting this initiative off the ground, and when we went live, we all celebrated with zest. However, soon after I realized that not much had changed in the practices of our operational colleagues. That entire vision of becoming a data driven department was not really coming to life. This setback was a key lesson learned, true across all sorts of digital projects, but especially relevant to business intelligence initiatives. There is a huge challenge when it comes to adoption, usage and hence achieving the larger vision of becoming an insights driven enterprise. There is a difference between what people say they need, versus what they actually need and will use. In addition, the digital experts love to dabble in all the new technologies which the field of business intelligence has been perpetually doling out. This combination is lethal and, in my experience, the root cause of most business intelligence initiatives not delivering adequate value. It is absolutely critical to spend time, effort and money into getting the organizational culture ready for shifting the basis of decision-making from intuition to a combination of data, analytics and intuition. It is an imperative to involve the leadership and immerse them into this new world of analytics, through engagement as well as possibly site visits and interactions with enterprises or individuals who have practical experience in this transition. The work practices need to be examined well before the technology gets implemented.

The leadership team needs to lead by example. For example, in a real estate company, we started the business intelligence programme, with the executive digital dashboard. The CEO and I mandated that from a certain day all PowerPoints were out, and all executive team meetings will be run using the digital dashboard. This set the cat among the pigeons and sent a clear message that the change was not optional. Even if the data was not perfect initially, and there were some teething issues in the ExCom, it sent a strong message that business and digital teams need to update the data properly in the core business systems and use the tools provided. The fact that the executive committee was embracing this change and driving it really helped the adoption down the line. Although my primary domain experience has been aviation, I have had the good fortune of also experiencing short stints in a few more businesses such as real estate, hospitality, entertainment and media. Real estate is perhaps the least digitized among these. Hence, for the CEO of this company to take such a strong, decisive step was quite exemplary.

The other facet about business intelligence programmes is the veracity of the data. This is a huge problem which needs to be solved, before value can accrue. As I said earlier, janitorial work over data is the most important piece of work in your business intelligence journey. In my experience, this is also the most ignored. The lack of quality of data is mostly due to deeply engrained business practices where short-term convenience in organizational silos takes preference over potential for strategic value to the whole enterprise. To give you a concrete example, sales leads are valuable data points for any enterprise. In the large enterprise context, you want AI algorithms to classify leads based on their propensity to convert into a sale. That way, the enterprise can focus their sales effort on those leads which have a high conversion propensity, thereby optimizing the sales funnel using advanced analytics. However, to do this downline initiative right, someone somewhere in the enterprise has to ensure that leads data is properly entered into a transactional system. If your call centre gets a lead, then the call centre agent needs to ensure that the full attributes of the lead are entered into their system. If your pre-sales team is entering the leads data, then they need to ensure quality input into sales tools such as salesforce. However, a call centre agent is hyper busy and measured on call volumes and call durations, so they just want to enter the very basic information and move on to the next call. The pre-sales or sales agent is not really digital savvy, so they are the least interested in entering data and more tuned to their coffee sessions with customers. The end result is low quality data on leads at the source itself and hence inability for algorithms down the line to be effective.

In the above scenario, the digital teams will typically focus on ensuring that the leads data from your call centre and salesforce system enters a data lake properly, ready for consumption by propensity predicting AI models. However, that is just not good enough. They need to work tirelessly, well before a cool AI can be brought into play, to ensure that data is corrected at source and legacy practices engrained over so many years, changed. That is a key role of your data and AI teams. It is not just about writing the cool AI algorithms.

The transactional phase of my career was the most important foundational steppingstone. And these phases are not sequential. For example, there is a still a fair component of transactional delivery in my role today. In fact, if you remove the shine from fancy words such as digital transformation, and go deeper into the root, you will find a key transactional digital system being delivered to automate a business process. Hence, it is important for those aspiring to digital transformation roles to spend a number of years in their career, digging into the world of transactional system delivery, getting their hands dirty and learning the trade at grassroots level. This grassroots knowledge will go a long way in facing off with the challenges which you will inevitably encounter in the journey of transformation.

Digital–strategic

The second phase of my digital career was focused on the strategic aspects of technology implementations, with the scope being the entire enterprise, as opposed to specific functional areas. This gave me a new perspective on how technology can be deployed in a much more planned manner, with a wider and sustainable impact, over a longer period of time.

Enterprise architecture

One of the key strategic disciplines in digital is enterprise architecture. I had the good fortune of developing this discipline from scratch within a large enterprise and learn through both setbacks and successes. The main idea of enterprise architecture is to look at the current and future deployments of digital and examine whether it is being done based on a proper blueprint. Alternatively, as I have found in most legacy enterprises, the architecture has just evolved, which experts refer to as 'accidental architecture'.

The field of solution architecture, which involves preparing the blueprint for a specific digital project, is of course quite evolved and you will find a solution architect being part of most digital projects. What is typically missing is enterprise architecture.

The discipline involves having a strategic overlay, over the digital projects as well as existing applications, to get a view from an enterprise perspective. For example, typical questions you are asked at the board or executive level are: 'What is our digital maturity?'; 'Are all our critical business areas automated?'; 'Which areas still need automation?'. In order to answer these questions, I have typically used the business capability model.

The business capability map

You first represent your entire enterprise in a business capability map. There are multiple ways you can draw up this capability map – customer centric capabilities, process centric capabilities or just existing business divisions. Select one and get a move on. I have preferred the customer centric capability map. You need to ensure that the Level 1 capability map is not more than 20–25 capabilities and Level 2 around 100. This level of abstraction reduces the complexity and then you can have an executive level viewpoint and dialogue over it.

Once the capability map has been drawn up, we need to overlay the current digital assets on top of that capability. This will pictorially give a view on which digital assets have been used to automate which business capability. The enterprise architects then work with the relevant digital business domain colleagues to provide the RAG, i.e., the red, amber, green, assessment of the level of digitization for each business capability. The assessment is predominantly about the number and efficacy of digital assets implemented for each business capability. In my experience, you can make this assessment very scientific and quantifiable; however,

I am not much of a fan of taking this scientific approach. I have preferred to get the relevant architects, business and analyst colleagues in a room, run a Delphi and, based on certain simple parameters, collectively decide the RAG assessment for digitization of each capability. This Delphi method yields a good enough assessment for an enterprise level, strategic dialogue to happen. Please remember that this is not an accounting exercise, and we need not aim for precision.

The capability map overlaid with current digital assets and then colour-coded to indicate level of maturity can help guide several important decisions and enterprise decisions. For example, it should definitely feed into deciding which business areas need digitization and investments. The digital team can have a dialogue with the exec teams on prioritization of digital investments and which areas, though not digitized, are ok to continue manual. It should feed into the portfolio planning process where you decide which digital projects should be run, to cover any gaps identified through the business capability model. Another typical question that the execs in any large enterprise will ask is: 'What is the roadmap for digitization?' This is the 'when' question. Once the portfolio of projects has been agreed, the enterprise architecture will typically lay this into a timeline view, over 2–3 years. This then shows the overall roadmap of digital delivery over a more longer-term environment.

Without this view, an overall context of the state of digitization is lacking. This typical deliverable of the enterprise architecture discipline clearly lays out the enterprise in terms of its business capabilities, overlays the current state of digitization on this capability map, both in terms of the digital assets as well as the assessment of the level of maturity, creates a portfolio or projects based on a cross-functional dialogue with exec stakeholders on investment priorities and then maps the projects in a 2–3-year timeline roadmap. When done and maintained properly, this is a

great asset for the enterprise. In fact, in my experience, just the
first artefact, i.e., laying the enterprise down in a business capability map, in itself is very valuable. It is rare to see the entire enterprise
represented in a single piece of paper. This map can also be overlaid with many other views which are not digital, for example
enterprise risk, allowing a structured dialogue and decision-
making on these topics.

Enterprise architecture, using tools like the capability map,
makes a contribution to helping enterprises with 'doing the right
things'. However, it also has a significant contribution to 'doing the
right things'. In large enterprises, in absence of a robust architecture discipline, there is significant duplication in digital assets. For
example, inevitably you will find multiple document management
systems across the aviation business. In some cases, where the
enterprise has grown through acquisitions, you may even find
multiple ERPs. A key deliverable of enterprise architects is to draw
up the framework to have proper reviews of these possible duplica-
tions and then take decisions in a structured, informed manner. In
my experience, this is best achieved by forming an architecture
review board, comprising solution architects from the various digital teams supporting the business, including relevant business
stakeholders in the board, and then having formal reviews on the
topic of digital asset standardization in this community. I have
experienced a spectrum of architecture-led standardization drives
in large enterprises – a spectrum ranging from brutal standardization to accidental standardization. In this case, I really believe a
balanced approach works best. The fact is that the enterprise world
of digital is becoming consumerized, hence staff expect to be
provided a level of choice in their business life, as much as they get
on their digital life, using their iPhones and downloading apps at
will. A brutal standardization effort at all levels of the digital landscape does not work, and neither does allowing an iPhone level
flexibility on downloading what you like. The enterprise architect

needs to provide a framework which allows for balanced decisions on this front. To give you a concrete example, in the business intelligence toolset, we have a choice of multiple tools for visualizations as well as tools required to get the data right, in the enterprise data lake. In my experience, an architect should spend time and effort in standardizing the back-end stack in the case of business intelligence, but allow some flexibility in terms of the visualization tools. In the case of business intelligence, that is a good balancing act.

Technical debt

One of the key reasons large enterprises cannot move as fast as their younger, start-up brethren has got to do with technical debt. Due to lack of architecture or lack of investment or just plain incompetence or a composite of factors, large enterprises have a number of legacy components in their current digital landscape. These legacy components accumulate over time, convert into significant legacy debt and clog the processes of the enterprise. One of the key responsibilities of the enterprise architect is to unclog the veins of an enterprise by slowly and surely eliminating this legacy debt. This, in my experience, is a very difficult task. The reason technical debt existss is because the enterprise is firstly not aware, and if they are, someone has not been able to find the investment needed to get rid of the debt. Hence, the enterprise architect is not going to have a magic wand to solve this issue. In my experience, there are two mantras that work on getting some traction on technical debt. Firstly, make it a part of your digital KPIs. It is a big obstacle to any transformation outcomes, so relevant stakeholders need to be made aware and it needs to be measured. Ensure that your large budget items, such as cloud transformation programmes, or applications enhancement budgets, block aside a significant investment to refactor the existing digital assets and modernize them. It is highly unlikely, in my opinion, that you will be able to get to the ideal state of building a dedicated business case for modernizing your digital assets per se. This is what architects sometimes get stuck with and then time is lost in trying to convince both CFOs as well as the business to sign off of the business case, mostly with no positive outcome. Instead, bake refactoring into your larger work programs and budgets and slowly start getting some traction on reducing the legacy.

The role of the enterprise architect

I have found that the enterprise architect role is one of the most difficult ones to fill. Hence, it is important that you get a suitable candidate for the head of enterprise architecture role. I had the good fortune of experiencing multiple personas for this role and have learned key pros and cons of each persona. One of the first heads I heard was excellent at conceptualizing and creating enterprise level models, which can become valuable assets for an enterprise, e.g., the business capability map. However, the problem with this persona was that the ability to then engage with a myriad of stakeholder groups, to use these models as a means towards a dialogue and then decisions, was missing. Hence, the architecture discipline became seen as a discipline which creates 'pretty pictures' but does not really add any value to the business. The second persona I experienced was someone extremely technical, who had grown through the technical ranks, into solution architect and then finally enterprise architect. This persona is able to manage the digital team, especially the engineering/tech talent, extremely well and immediately finds a following in this stakeholder group. However, a key function of the architecture discipline is to bridge the gap between business and digital. A setback I experienced with this second persona was the ability to drive a number of the strategic outcomes I listed earlier and help bridge the traditional gap that typically exists between tech and business teams. The persona I have seen work really well, was someone who had that gravitas and influence to have difficult but important discussions, with senior stakeholders, but also has the depth to have a deep technical discussion with the tech talent in digital. This persona relies on the just enough architecture principle to ensure artefacts are created for a business outcome and purpose, not just optics or because enterprise architecture frameworks suggest that we should. I had two such architects head up this function in my career. Both of them had an excellent ability to influence and converse with senior stakeholders. I think this is crucially important. Enterprise architecture is not a back-office function. The head has a clear responsibility to deal with business stakeholders and drive consensus around difficult topics such as investments in reducing technical debt, standardization versus choice, reuse and digital investment with the future in mind, as opposed to only for resolving current issues. Hence, in my experience, influence without authority is the most important competence for this role. We need to get that one right. Then, of course, comes the specialist technical knowledge, which is also key to ensuring that there is a strong foundation to the strategic choices the enterprise architecture role helps enable. And finally, this role has to have the ability to abstract things out, ideally using architectural frameworks, so that there can be a dialogue with non-technical stakeholders on aspects where technology has a strategic business impact. As you build this discipline within your enterprise, please ensure you keep a sharp focus and vigil on your architecture teams being focused on business value and outcomes, as sometimes they can get carried away and lost in their own worlds of blueprints, models and pretty pictures.

Driving innovation

Technology initiated or led innovation is another area of digital which has a strategic scope. I built and then ran the innovation program, on multiple occasions, under the digital umbrella. There are multiple views on the topic of innovation and much deliberation in the enterprise world on this subject. Some executives will opine that innovation is everyone's business and they resist any structured approaches to instilling innovation into the enterprise culture. Some go the other way and set up innovation labs, allocate a budget, appoint a team and ask them to drive innovation within the enterprise. In my experience, a structured approach to innovation is important to get the enterprise to start thinking differently.

At the very foundational level, I have run 'tech matters!' or 'digital matters!' sessions on a monthly basis. This gives the digital team an opportunity to converse with the larger staff base on digital topics and also reinforces our view that in today's era, digital matters and people should take the time out and energy to engage with it. One of the mantras for success is to make these sessions and their agenda quite intriguing, so that they evoke a sense of curiosity among colleagues. For instance, the standard agenda for one such session I used to run was as follows:

a Start-up

b From the CDO's desk

c Four tricks

d Future matters!

e Maker lab

f Q&A

The topics we selected every month, also had cryptic topics such as 'connecting the dots' or 'around the bend'. It is rare to find a digital update or awareness session having such topics and agendas. However, this was very intentional. One of the important ingredients of innovation culture is a perpetual sense of curiosity. I wanted colleagues to feel a deep sense of intrigue when they got these personalized invites from me, for these sessions, and then join in, together into this journey of unknown.

One of the most innovative sessions I have run involved engaging with over 200 colleagues from all walks of life, with professions ranging from chefs to radio disc jockeys, in a mass coding session. Most of them had never seen an integrated development environment (IDE) in their lives or written a single piece of code. The objective of this session was to demystify coding and explain how the world of software engineering had become about reuse and modularity. In addition, we also wanted our colleagues to feel that feeling of creative accomplishment which our coders feel each time the code they have written produces an outcome on the screen. I asked one of my data scientists to write a cloud-based code, which would produce a personalized piece of art based on some input that the function would receive from the user. We hosted this function on the cloud, assessable to the world. After having gone through the agenda items on the 'digital matters!' session, when we reached the 'maker lab' agenda item, I unveiled to the 200 colleagues who were attending that today all of us would write a piece of code and execute it. Although online, I could almost feel the heightened buzz among the audience. Then I got our data scientist online and he led the process of writing code, slowly, one small step at a time. All 200 colleagues did exactly what he asked them to, including opening a cloud IDE, writing seven lines of code, one of which involved invoking the function that our data scientist had written and then hosted on the cloud. Once the coding was done, I asked all colleagues to take a deep breath and on the count of three, press the Run button on their IDEs.

You can well imagine the extreme excitement as 200 colleagues saw a beautiful artform pop up on their computer – individualized art based on some input they had entered in *their* code. Innovation hit home to all of them that day. There is no more powerful way to imbibe innovation, other than getting people to experience it first hand, ideally based on actions they perform. That was the objective of the maker lab section on our agenda.

As I awaited their reaction, I saw excitement-driven virality in action. Within a few minutes, the chat window of our live virtual session was abuzz with posts of the artforms from our colleagues. And there were virtual high fives and claps all around us. I later got to hear about colleagues sharing stories with their families on how they had created their first piece of code, which yielded a beautiful artform. I am sure this form of innovation goes a long way in sharping the innovation culture in large enterprises, as opposed to attending conferences or hearing keynotes throughout long days in fancy beach resorts.

Besides this foundational engagement, I believe nurturing a robust innovation ecosystem is quite important for large enterprises. I have covered the details in Chapter 3, *Working the Honeycomb – digital capabilities*; however, the digital team should consider building multiple nodes of this ecosystem, including but not limited to: university engagements whereby students can participate in delivering innovation projects sponsored by the enterprise; structured engagement with digital partners on innovations in their field of expertise; periodic immersion visits to places where the participants can actually touch and feel the disruptive ideas in action; hackathons, both internal to the enterprise and external; participation in innovation incubators and accelerators; and deep engagement with the start-up world, including venture capitalists.

Broadly, the above allows a structured engagement with ideas which are in (a) Horizon 3 – far out ideas, five-plus years away from reality, typically with universities and students; (b) Horizon 2 – ideas not yet implemented or near horizon ideas, typically with accelerators, incubators and start-ups; and then, of course (c) Horizon 1 – ideas ready for deployment which typically result from engagement internally and events such as hackathons. In my experience, enterprises need a structured way to engage with this ecosystem rather than just hoping that innovative mindset will evolve organically without much effort. There is so much focus within enterprises to run existing operations, and that is rightly so, given the current P&L is dependent upon this focus. Executives, managers, front-line staff are burning long hours delving into the current state of affairs, the current processes, the current challenges to ensure the current set of outcomes are achieved. There are multiple governance committees providing oversight on this current situation and any deviations are immediately highlighted and immediate action demanded in multiple executive forums. Everyone is under pressure in the current context. Hence, innovation is really not anyone's agenda. One day, a disrupter is born in a garage and launches an all-out attack on the enterprise's business model, utilizing a technology that all enterprise executives concluded as a fad. Once the executives sense this is happening, they immediately get panicky and use multiple random methods to make innovation and digital among the top three focus areas of their enterprise. However, in my opinion and experience, by that time it is too late, and decline will typically set in. I believe that a proactive, structured approach to managing innovation helps get the curiosity, learning and experimentation bug, slowly seep into the organization's ethos. As a consequence of this deeper shift in mindset, innovation automatically becomes a top agenda item for the enterprise, helping the enterprise to have a healthy mix of fixing the basics and investing in the future.

Core platforms and systems

At the heart of any larger enterprise, you will inevitably find a set of core platforms, which have been procured from a third-party, typically a large technology provider. For example, the Aviation business has several of these platforms. The core reservation and check-in system is mostly third-party procured from one of two large aviation IT providers, Amadeus or Sabre. Aviation has a number of other third-party software for specialist areas such as flight planning and dispatch, crew rostering and management, etc. Hospitality has at their core property management systems (PMS) as well as distribution systems, again procured from big players such as Oracle. Real estate businesses typically have systems such as Yardi running their core real estate management functions. Manufacturing businesses typically implement ERP systems such as SAP as their core platforms. These core systems are critical both tactically, as there is a key dependency on them, as well as strategically, because if they do not evolve and innovate constantly, enterprise ability to innovate will also be hampered.

Typically, in the transactional world of digital, disciplines such as supplier or vendor management help manage the operational aspects of these core platforms as well help manage the vendors who deliver these services. For example, these disciplines will chase service levels and ensure the vendor meets them and if not, they ensure contractual penalties are exercised. All this work is good and an important aspect of digitizing enterprises. However, we live in an increasingly networked world. Very rarely all the capabilities needed by an enterprise to deliver its mission and promise to its customers can be built organically. Hence, there is a deep reliance on a network of vendors to deliver the mission. In the world of digital, this reliance on a network of partners is even more accentuated, given they run the core platforms which run mission critical enterprise processes. Hence, in my experience, it is critical to go well beyond the discipline of vendor management and embrace partnership or ecosystem manager as a discipline.

The key mantra behind this new discipline is to nurture a deeper, strategic partnership with your core vendor ecosystem. A strategic overlay of vendor relationships allows the enterprise to shape the product roadmap of their core digital products, ensure knowledge sharing between these top partners and the enterprise and participation in the innovation funnels of the partners. If such a relationship is well nurtured, enterprises will inevitably also get better response and support from their vendors at the operational level. I have formally established a partnership management process within digital and assigned it to one of my digital leadership team members. A formal framework and cadence is then established for partnership management. This firstly involves setting up a formal governance structure between partner and enterprise digital as well as business executives. During these meetings, the agenda should clearly cover much more than just SLAs and services credits. It is good for the enterprise to share their portfolio roadmaps with the partners, so that they have a clear view on the priorities of the enterprise. Sometimes, enterprises treat their project portfolios as trade secrets! I believe it is important to engage with your partners on what you are planning to do in the future, openly and proactively, so that they can contribute to delivering that future. Of course, partners will have a sales mindset and want to position their products, but then there are enough controls within large enterprises to not get swayed by their pitches and ensure due diligence when it comes to product selections.

Developing and nurturing relationships

The other important aspect of partnership management is just to develop deep relationships with key executives. For some of the key technology products, the development and senior executives are typically in the US. Hence, having that hook into their corporate HQs and nurturing those relationships is quite important. When it comes to flexibility on commercials, in any case all regional offices go to their corporate office for approvals. Hence, if you have nurtured a relationship with a partner executive in the Silicon Valley, that always helps. Product development is typically led from the HQs, while the delivery is mostly in software centres in India. Hence, if you want your requirements to be catered in the next release, that relationship with HQ will come in handy. In my experience, this shift from vendor to partner management, if taken beyond the semantics, has several strategic benefits for the enterprise. It is definitely worth spending the time and effort in crafting a clear framework for partnership management and then ensuring the right leader in your team is given this portfolio to manage.

Conclusion

My experience in the transactional aspects of digital gave me a sound grounding on the foundations. This is an essential first step in a digital career path. The second stint was a deep dive into the strategic aspects of digital, which is again a crucial next step, as it gave me wider lens on the scope and impact of digital, wider both from an organizational point of view, as well as a wider time horizon. This prepared me well for the third phase of my career, which is the fascinating world of digital being deployed for the purpose of an authentic transformation.

A large part of my experience in the world of digital transformation has been encapsulated in the Honeycomb approach, which I have described at length earlier in this book. Hence, I will cover two areas here, where I believe we need to lay emphasis to accelerate the digital transformation within legacy enterprises. First and foremost is to get established legacy enterprises to realize that true transformation has to do with business models. There is no doubt that these enterprises need to turbo charge their digitizing efforts, as there is significant opportunity for revenue generation, cost saving and enhancing customer experience within the boundaries of their existing business models. This needs to be done and the digital teams need to ensure there is focus on digitizing an enterprise. Having said that, just digitizing an enterprise, in my view, is not digital transformation. It is important, no doubt, but not enough. The rubber of accelerating transformation hits the road when enterprises open up their minds to the opportunities of exploring new business models. I have been part of large enterprises where over 100 million customer records with first party data are available to be cleaned up and then converted into a true digital asset, on which new business models can be conceived and scaled. Just think about that a minute. If you are a venture capitalist-backed start-up, that level of customer insight will immediately make your customer acquisition cost (CAC) KPIs amazingly attractive and you will find a whole lot of funding to help build your disruptive business model. However, in an established enterprise, this gold mine of data is mostly ignored.

Executives typically grow through the ranks of the specific business domain, e.g., aviation, banking, retail, etc., so they are just not comfortable in launching new business models, which by their very essence will not be from their industry. This executive mindset is a huge barrier to business model diversification. My enthusiastic war cry: 'Look! You have a gold mine of 100 million customer records. Just imagine what you could do with that!' has often fallen on deaf, bemused executive ears. Meanwhile, digital natives such as Amazon, Alibaba and numerous others have shed this inhibition of belonging to a particular industry and just used their internal capabilities and mindset to rule over multiple industry segments. A key task of digital leaders is to get this mindset shift in established organizations so that it can see the potential of leveraging their legacy to launch and scale new business models. I don't see any reason why multiple business models cannot be booted up within established enterprises, leveraging excellent assets such as data, brand and trust that they engender for years in their customer base. The growth of 'embedded finance' as a new business model is testament to the potential of doing exactly this and embedding financial business models, inside traditional industry players such as retail, or aviation. Financial products such as Buy Now Pay Later, which is basically a credit product, is now widely available on a number of e-commerce retail players, which embed the capability of a Fintech in their e-commerce journeys and create a new revenue line from their existing customer base. I see the same logic which gave birth to 'embedded finance' giving rise to a number of other embedded business models, namely 'embedded retail' and 'embedded healthcare', where customer journeys are interspersed with curated offers from these industries and new revenue streams created for the established enterprise.

I believe getting momentum on new business models within established enterprises is one of the most difficult things to do in digital transformation. In order to ease the change, I suggest a phased process for running these initiatives. This is very similar to the start-up world where they start with angel funding to conduct some initial research, followed by seed funding for developing a minimum viable product (MVP) and so on to Series E and beyond, when the new venture is fully scaled and ready for exit. Similarly, in established enterprises, a small fund should be set aside for digital teams to conduct experimentation and MVP on various embedded digital models. These MVPs are typically enabled on the enterprise's website or app, as embedded use cases, for example, Buy Now Pay Later credit lines within a retail or aviation e-commerce website. These MVPs then need to be watched and monitored for uptake and growth KPIs, and those business models which see clear traction can then be funded further, until they scale and can be considered of exiting as a completely new venture.

Often during my experience of pushing the business model agenda as a key pillar of digital transformation, I have been asked why an enterprise should not just focus on it knitting, and getting that right, rather than foray into these new areas. My view on this is quite firm. To me, there is no authentic digital transformation if the opportunity of digital business models is not explored. Period. For one, your knitting may become irrelevant in the digital era, as we have seen with so many traditional business models, such as brick and mortar retail. And, perhaps more importantly, there is a

huge *opportunity* cost of you not pursuing business model experimentation, just because it is too difficult to do or indeed you have
these traditional, rather romantic views of sticking to your knitting. You owe it to your stakeholders to use your vast resources
and brand power to extend your reach into new digital businesses
that not only give a huge P&L upside but also a valuation uptick,
which is not possible when you continue to pursue a strategy of
organic growth with traditional business models. It is incumbent,
and in my view a core responsibility of digital professionals, to do
the hard work and experience the sweat and toil required to go
after these significant opportunities, rather than taking the easy
path of just fixing the basics in digitizing existing business models.

The second area in transformation journeys which needs a
special mention and contributes to acceleration is digital mindset
or culture. Like new business models, a culture change is another
mission impossible. However, just because it is difficult it does not
mean it is not important and can be ignored. In my opinion, no
mindset change, no transformation, period.

I was part of the internal brand council for one of the world's
premier brands. We were being guided by a brand consultancy
based out of Europe and with their help we built a new brand
positioning and motto for the external world. I remember so
vividly when we were told that for the new brand to live outside,
it first needs to be fully embraced internally and for the new brand
to live internally, we need to run internal movements which align
and associate with the new brand positioning. A culture change is
very similar. To ensure that a new culture is embraced internally,
we need to run a whole internal movement that aligns with the
new values you want people to imbibe. When I say internal movement, it cannot be done in the case of digital mindset in another
way, but a movement of action – a movement of doing stuff in the
new ways that you want the company to adopt. There is not much
point putting posters on walls at the start of this process. Just get

on and do stuff in new ways. For example, if an attribute of your digital mindset is speed, work with a few executives, baseline 'time to decide' on key processes owned by them and then speed these decisions up by a factor of x. Measure the time to decide KPI and once you are sure there has been an improvement, celebrate the result and yes, at this stage, put posters on the walls to celebrate the outcome.

If your digital mindset attribute is adaptability, get a few willing executives to run their business processes using agile methods. Conduct daily stand-ups for these processes, make videos of the buzz created when teams work together in an interactive, collaborative manner using some of the tools of the agile method. I have experience of doing this with a very traditional HR team of a large enterprise – not digital or technology, but the HR team. When other departments heard that HR was running some of their critical projects using agile, it created curiosity. We then asked the HR team members to share their actions and not just words with their colleagues, which got them excited and wanting to join in. If your digital mindset attribute is co-create, then run your next big project in collaboration with teams from completely different fields. Invite diverse perspectives and people to co-create the outcomes with you. As I had shared earlier, I had experience of inviting students, experts from alien industries and partners into some of our key projects and that brought this concept of co-creation to life.

When it comes to culture, only actions go viral. Culture is indeed a derived variable. You cannot impact it directly, no matter what consultants tell or sell to you. You need to create an internal movement of action to get the culture to come alive and scale in established enterprises. As covered in the Honeycomb approach, there are a number of other things that digital leaders need to do, in order to lead, deliver and accelerate an authentic transformation in established organizations. However, doing the hard yards with business model transformation and culture change are two of the important aspects, in my experience, to accelerate this transformation journey.

As I reflect on my three decades' worth of experience in the world of digital, I can encapsulate it into these three phases: transaction, strategic and transformation. These phases were not sequential and there are significant overlaps among them. There are significant learnings which one phase contributes to the other. This is another reason I do not believe in the dogma of two-speed IT, where transactional work is conducted by one team and the interesting, transformation work by another. I see these work items as part of a single whole, which when done right ultimately leads to driving successful transformation within established enterprises. Hence, in my experience, a unified approach across these three dimensions works best, when augmented with a unified team, aligned and focused on one mission, the mission of transformation and its exponential potential and outcomes.

I am not done yet with this world of transformation. I am sure there are many more curves and learnings ahead. However, I hope that you have gleaned some takeaways from my reflections on the career and sunset gone by, as we all prepare for the beautiful world of disruption and opportunity ahead of us, accelerating and rising with the sunshine in the horizon.

INDEX

Note: Page numbers in *italics* refer to figures